THE MISSING BUSINESS INSTRUCTIONS

How to safely navigate the hazards
of growing your business!

By Tim Rylatt & Henry Laker

The Missing Business Instructions

How to safely navigate the hazards
of growing your business!

ISBN 978-1-914076-10-7 (paperback)

ISBN 978-1-914076-11-4 (ebook)

Editing and typesetting: preparetopublish.com

CONTENTS

FOREWORD

This book has been written for you, the backbone of our society – the business owners!

It's been written because being a business owner can be one of the most rewarding roles on the planet but equally, can also be one of the toughest jobs in the universe.

The highs are so very high, but the lows are so very, very low.

Having been a business coach for 12 years at the time of writing this book, and as a business owner myself, I have experienced the joy of success, and the fear and frustration of failure.

I have seen this not just in my own companies but also across a wide range of clients and others in the broader business community.

The difference between success and failure often originates well before either actually happen. This is the case because both these outcomes arrive based on the cumulative result of many minor missteps and not because of one great or poor decision.

WHY DO WE MAKE SO MANY MISTAKES AS BUSINESS OWNERS?

The vast majority of us believe we are better than average.

...and that is both fundamentally impossible and a dangerous delusion!

Note that I used the word *'believe'*, not *'think'*.

It's an important distinction as it requires a lot more reflection and willingness to challenge a belief than it does a thought.

This has become recognised as a real psychological condition known as the Dunning Kruger effect, if you are minded to learn more!

Essentially, it creates a different challenge to the one most business owners believe they have.

They think that the issue is simply a matter of **knowing** more (as they already view themselves as competent with existing knowledge), but the reality is that often we actually haven't yet used what we know very effectively.

The problem is compounded if you don't believe that this need exists. It simply means you are much less likely to apply the correct solution!

Rather than acknowledging that the problem is within, you seek for an answer outside.

The classic break-up line of 'It's not you, it's me' actually would be rather more true!

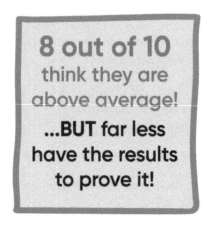

8 out of 10 think they are above average!

...BUT far less have the results to prove it!

With this in mind, the biggest single factor I have identified that drives success for business owners is a true willingness to objectively review themselves and their business performance, and then to act positively upon what that reveals.

This process often benefits or is prompted by the perspective of someone outside the business owner's own head, who can provide qualified and realistic insight.

Once the honest appraisal has been accepted, a voracious pursuit of knowledge, action, and mindset improvement by the business owner themselves can make a huge difference to the rate of, and level of success resulting.

A person with a true growth mindset draws on all relevant sources of wisdom and support, whilst someone with a closed mindset looks mainly inwardly for answers from their own available experience and knowledge.

To coin a quote from the great Ken Blanchard (author of the One Minute Manager series):

'None of us is as smart as all of us.'

When you read this book, my challenge to you is to keep an open mind and to view every item you spot that relates to a gap or current issue for you as a win.

It means you have discovered an opportunity, and if you couple that opportunity with an intention and an action to grasp it... well, the world's your oyster!

Chapter 1

THE MISSING BUSINESS INSTRUCTIONS

Most people in business are on a journey.

Robert Kiyosaki (author of *Rich Dad, Poor Dad*) summarised this as four stages of development. The employed, self-employed, business owner, and investor.

➤ The employed exchange their time and expertise for the money of their employer.

➤ The self-employed 'own their own job' and exchange their time for the company's money.

➤ The business owner 'owns a system' which is operated by themselves or their employees.

➤ The investor makes money from money.

The most common misconception is that the self-employed person thinks of themselves as a business owner, but in reality they are still required by their company. If they are absent for any substantial period of time, the cracks start to appear, and the company performance starts to decline or crumble.

I mention this in our first chapter here as there is a reason why this happens, and it has to do with a sense of self-perception and self-worth that the self-employed adopt.

There is a certain social prestige in being a business owner. It is viewed with a degree of respect and is often seen as a step above employment.

However, it is also the case that many business owners who are actually sitting in the self-employed category are working long hours for little income and a whole lot of stress.

This is because the skills to do a job are complementary to, but wholly different to the skills required to grow a business.

Whilst almost everyone who is employed receives training, guidance, and support to become competent, then capable, and lastly expert in their role, almost no business owners receive formal training or instruction on how to build a profitable, efficient, and successful business.

I term this gap in guidance as being 'The Missing Business Instructions'.

When you think back to your childhood, it's likely that you (or perhaps a sibling or friend) at some point tried to build a model. This may have been an Airfix model, Lego, Meccano, or from another brand, but one thing was universal:

The packaging came with a clear image of the finished model, and along with the individual parts, you received a set of visual instructions that told you the sequence of steps and the related tools to use to construct your model.

When that wasn't present, or when tools or components were missing, it became a whole lot more challenging, and it almost certainly ended up in failure or giving up.

Well, when it comes to business, in most cases there are no instructions provided.

You have to work out what to do when, and in many instances, you have no idea what tool would be best to apply at each stage. It's also quite likely that several critical pieces are missing!

This is the challenge that business owners across the world face when they set out, and it is compounded by the Dunning Kruger effect (explained in the Foreword) when the new 'business owner' believes that the skillset and knowledge they have gained from having had an employed role in the industry sector is sufficient for operating and growing a business.

Add in the fact that this confusion about reality is almost universal, and it becomes more of a challenge!

You see, too many business owners judge the success of their business by the other business owners that directly surround them.

They take 'average' as the benchmark for success, rather than looking at the top 5% of performance in their sector.

Many also assess this by comparison with their wage in employment, rather than the potential for profit that their company and marketplace can offer.

What that leads to is a situation where doing just a little better than the average becomes the aspiration, rather than shooting for the stars.

It's very common for business owners to say, 'We're doing well, we achieved about the same as last year', and 'We are not *un*comfortable'.

However, the absence of substantial pain is not the same as success.

In any other field of endeavour, achieving the same outcome as last year would be called 'plateauing' and would indicate a slowdown in progress and perhaps hitting the limit of current understanding and capability... and the problem with plateauing is that some competitors won't. It's easy to catch up to someone who isn't moving forward.

The need to push on, develop, and move is always there in business. You either grow or you die, ultimately.

The first question you need to ask yourself, with a suitable level of objectivity, is:

'Where is my business now?'

Here are five categories that can help you put a name to your situation. It's ok to state that you are between two stages if you are unsure.

Business Development Stages

Where is your business on this scale right now?

STARTING OUT	SELF-EMPLOYED	SCALING BUSINESS	OWNER INDEPENDENCE	INVESTOR
You are building a new business	Your business operates functionally	Your business performance and results amplify	Your business is not reliant on you	You exit the business
Low earning	Modest earning	High earning	Passive income	Capital payout

Chapter 1 – Reflection and Exercise

When I compare myself versus my peers, I feel that our current level of business expertise is:

➤ Better than most?

➤ Average?

➤ Worse than most?

I feel this way because:

....

....

....

....

When I compare myself versus my peers, I feel that our current level of business success and rewards is:

➤ Better than most?

➤ Average?

➤ Worse than most?

I feel this way because:

....

....

....

....

Chapter 2

THE BUSINESS STAR

Within this book we'll be looking at ten main areas of your business. The framework that covers these aspects is called '**The Business Star**'.

Whilst not all businesses are totally alike, and certainly every business owner has their own uniqueness, there *is* a suggested order to approach these topics in, and the numbers 1 to 10 on the diagram indicate this.

All ten areas are important, and none should be neglected too long or ignored to its detriment. Nearly all issues that arise in business stem from either a lack of focus or a lack of skill, systems, or diligence in one or more of these elements.

The ten elements within The Business Star are:

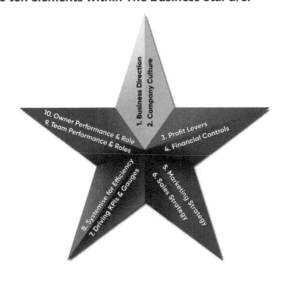

Over the course of the next ten chapters, I will guide you through each aspect and share with you some key insights.

You may be looking at this diagram and immediately shortlisting your priorities within your business. I'd ask that you hold off on the assumption of what's important for a little while yet and do that after reading all ten chapters. You may well be surprised at what is involved and what some of your options and strategies should be!

One point (excuse the pun) to note about the star diagram is the use of the colour green to highlight the first two categories. I have done this as these two fundamental aspects are essential for any truly aspirational business owner to grasp and apply. The direction you set together with the purpose and the definition of the people you want your culture to be formed around are essential.

The order of 'attack' suggested for you to use against the ten sections is not the only option, but it is my recommended approach, particularly for businesses that are relatively new or that have never undertaken this style of growth approach before.

The thinking behind the suggested approach is:

The direction is important because you need to know where you are and where you are going. It helps to know your intention before you make the first steps.

The culture defines who you are, why anyone should care, and what your team stands for. On your journey you will connect with lots of people: clients, teammates, suppliers, and others. Defining who you want to work with and how you want your company represented early makes it easier to achieve the right mix.

The outcome of any successful business includes a healthy and sustainable profit. The profit levers are the mechanism by which profit is generated and the strategic framework for boosting it. If you understand this early and have a plan that is focused upon it, those results are far more likely to actually happen.

Profit is only ever a paper exercise if the financial control and management of cashflow isn't successful. This is vital to grasp before pushing too hard on other elements. In fact, if you scale up whilst you have a cash gap or are losing money operationally due to a lack of control or understanding of these factors, it could actually prove fatal for your business!

Marketing and sales are the drivers of the business. Without clients you don't have a business... once you know that the business functionally makes a profit on its operations, then bringing up the volume of work to capacity (e.g. more clients, more orders, or larger-scale orders) is the next logical step.

The Driving KPIs are the metrics that allow you to accelerate your progress in any area of the company you choose, and the gauges are how these are reported and presented clearly. Understanding the 'drivers' in your business enables you to grow more efficiently and enables the profit compound effect (more on this later) to happen.

Systems are essential to business consistency and efficiency. Too many companies leave systemisation for later, but the premise is simple: consistency enables scaling and forecasting, and efficiency enables profit.

Team roles and performance underpin all of the above. It's essential to get the right people into the right positions, with the right skills and attitude. It's also important to show them a personal path forward and to invest time and effort into their development. Getting this right is a foundation for business autonomy and scaling up.

The owner's role and performance are the most overlooked elements of business growth. It is very helpful when targeting the growth, scaling, or exit from the company that you as the owner have defined the roles you currently fulfil and which ones you will continue with or replace in the next phase of business. Planning this in advance helps you to prioritise systemisation, training, recruitment, and your own time management.

As you can see, there is a natural clockwise rotation between these elements that interconnects.

Whilst it *is* certainly possible to leap from one aspect to another without this approach, it often leads to a more sporadic, less considered, and less successful outcome.

Chapter 2 – Reflection and Exercise

My current view is that my focus needs to be applied with the following percentage weighting on each element of The Business Star in the coming year...

My Focus (%)
(should add up to 100% overall)

Establishing Direction	____
Building Culture	____
Applying Profit Levers	____
Control of Finances	____
Marketing Strategy	____
Sales Strategy	____
KPIs	____
Systems	____
Team Performance	____
Owner Role	____

N.B. If you have more than one business owner, director, or other involved party, get each to complete the exercise. This can help you decide on and separate out overall responsibilities.

Chapter 3

STAGES OF BUSINESS DEVELOPMENT

Earlier on I referenced the progression stages that Robert Kiyosaki identified in his own very well-known and widely appreciated books.

The four stages referred to the individuals' 'staging' more than the companies themselves (employed, self-employed, business owner, and investor). This matched the underlying methodology he was defining for achieving personal wealth.

Businesses have a similar staging in terms of their development and the performance outcomes they deliver for their owners and shareholders.

➤ The four different stages are:

➤ Dysfunctional/Start-up

➤ Functional

➤ Scalable/Independence

➤ Saleable

Let's take each in turn.

A *dysfunctional* business is one that is either unprofitable, unreal, or fledgling.

Unprofitable is obvious: the maths simply isn't working, and that will sooner or later (if unresolved) lead to its demise.

Unreal is the less obvious version...

Normally, these business are surviving but often only due to the commitment and overwork of the business owners, their families, or staff. These companies are living on the edge and have little resilience in the event of any additional issues arising. If the owner gets sick, it may well be the end. The owners are often working for below minimum wage or significantly more hours than are normal for an employee.

The traits of these companies can vary, but often will include poor or highly inconsistent cashflow, unreasonable working hours or conditions that no employee would ever tolerate (but the business owner does), and a constant sense of tail chasing. Frequently this is accompanied by high staff turnover and a sense of high stress/constant emergency.

Fledgling businesses are simply at a very early stage and as such are still learning how to market, operate, and fulfil effectively.

There is often an equal sense of excitement and overload in these companies since (as almost all business owners will tell you) they often involve a huge amount of work and effort to launch. Fledgling businesses often have a tough time because everything is new, including the clients, the team, the systems, and the experience. The failure rate of new businesses is higher than at any other stage.

A *functional* business 'works' but still requires the owner to be directly and frequently involved. When this isn't the case, problems appear.

Functional businesses are almost always owner operated and tend to be quite small in scale. This is because the owner is still essential to the day-to-day running, and as the company grows, so too do their duties and the lengths of their days.

Many will find some work-arounds that allow for a degree of expansion, and even the creation of a management team and a staff structure that operates under their direct command... but they struggle to delegate effectively and are often heard to say, 'When I'm not involved, it doesn't work as well.'

Functional businesses are essentially sound and often successful in the sense that they can provide a good level of income for the owners and, with hard work, a better balance of work/home life than the dysfunctional stage.

BUT there *is* still that big elephant in the room...

The business only works as long as the owner is directly involved.

Many will get the company performing well enough to allow them a holiday (or several) throughout a year, but the growth is stunted or the company has some aspects that start to suffer if they are absent for too long.

They are the business hub, and it is reliant on them.

The obvious problem is that the scalability of a business that is largely reliant on one individual is limited. It can only grow to the level that the hours and energy of that person can handle. For some, that isn't too much of an issue as they are workaholics who love their position and role (and some deliberately make themselves indispensable for that reason!).

At least it isn't a problem all the time that they still feel that way...

The hidden problem with functional businesses is not in the day-to-day profitability of the company. In fact, many are profitable at a level where the owners are earning a few times the salary they would in an equivalent employed role. It comes in the valuation of the business as a whole and in its attractiveness as a buyable asset to investors.

This becomes a problem when the business owner starts to want different things for themself. It may be that they want to reduce their involvement or to sell the company overall. At this point, those reliance points become stifling, and often the corrective action required goes beyond the desired timeframe for the business owner.

A _scalable, independent_ business works well. It is a set of systems, well delivered by a skilled team with clear and distinct roles and responsibilities.

Businesses that are truly scalable are not reliant on any one individual. They almost certainly will benefit from excellent staff who are good at their jobs, but no-one is irreplaceable, and no one element is critical for survival or growth.

This is a massive step forward from a functional business. It is the transition from 'self-employment' into 'business ownership', and the critical factors are the removal of the reliance on the owner (or other person) and the development of systems.

The scalable aspect is linked to the ability for repetition – either within the existing business framework or as a totally separate entity elsewhere. A franchise is the very essence of this principle as it is simply a set of training resources, a set of systems, and the application in a suitable environment.

Having operated a franchise business personally for ten years, I can tell you that the quality of the training and the effectiveness of those systems can accelerate the success of a second, third, or even thousandth location and business entity. All you have to do is look at McDonalds restaurants to see the power of this idea.

A *saleable* business is simply a scalable, independent business prepared well for marriage. The core tenets are the same, but the presentation is different.

Saleability is based on a number of factors, but some of the critical ones are:

➤ Consistency of results

➤ Strength of existing client base/relationships

➤ Marketing and sales strategy

➤ Future profit confidence

➤ Other financial factors (e.g. stock/assets)

➤ Systemisation and employees

➤ Profile and brand reputation

➤ Independence/lack of reliance on the owner or other person.

A saleable business has prepared to present its case for maximum valuation and worked hard towards proving that argument. This preparation may well have taken between a few months and a few years and has the exclusive intention of bringing the owners the greatest capital return for the sale.

So why are we explaining these stages and separating the different types of business situation out?

Simple – if you know what the next step is, you can take the relevant next action.

The progression of a business is not instantaneous and needs to be considered. It is hard to go from dysfunctional to highly attractive for sale in one go: it's easier to eat an elephant one bite at a time.

By identifying where you are on the journey, and what the next stage of evolution is, you can make the appropriate step forward.

Many business owners get stuck on one aspect of their business, seeking perfection and finding themselves looping back to that issue time and again. In the same way as attending a gym and exercising only your right arm won't get your body fit as a whole, neither does a fixation on one element of a company.

Chapter 3 – Reflection and Exercise

When I look at my business *honestly*, I would say that today it is at the following stage of progression...

(tick as appropriate)

Dysfunctional/Start-up	❏
Functional	❏
Scalable/Independence	❏
Saleable	❏

I feel this way because...

....

....

....

....

The next big step I want to take in my business is:

....

....

....

....

DIRECTION

When you are looking to travel somewhere, it helps to know two things:

1. Where you are intending to get to

2. Where you are right now.

In fact, without either of these crucial pieces of information, it's highly unlikely that your journey will be successful.

Yet, in the vast majority of cases, business owners are unclear about either of these.

They either haven't defined their progression goals (short, medium, and long term) clearly enough or they are unclear on where they are now.

Sometimes this lack of clarity on the here and now can be partly delusional (remember the Dunning Kruger effect explained at the start of this book?).

So how do we make sure that your journey plan is set appropriately and with all the relevant information from the outset?

UNDERSTANDING 'HERE'

If I asked you to tell me where you are physically, right now, it's likely that you would be able to do so.

➤ You could describe the environment, the scenery, the buildings, or a range of other items... and you would not be wrong.

➤ You could tell me the precise latitude and longitude in degrees, minutes, and seconds... and you would not be wrong.

➤ You could simply tell me the postcode and the address... and you would not be wrong then either!

All of these answers are correct, and in part this makes the point I want neatly.

You see, when someone asks you where you are at in your business, there are many ways you could choose to answer that question, and none of them is wrong because the answer can be as broad as the question.

When we look at properly understanding and assessing our businesses with the intention of setting plans ahead, all too often we *default* to simply the financials because they are the most readily available evidence of performance.

This only gives *part* of the picture. The majority of financial reports show history only, and they often have been 'manipulated' by the accountant to present them in the best light for HMRC (Her Majesty's Revenue and Customs) and tax purposes. They are 'correct', but they are also 'misleading' in many instances.

A bit like the quiz show *'Catchphrase'*, where contestants are allowed to remove just one square at a time and have to guess what the whole picture is showing whilst only seeing some sections of the image... it's a lot easier when you have a more complete view!

That's not to say that targeting an improvement in turnover, margin, or profit is a bad idea (far from it); it just needs a bit more investigation on why those starting numbers exist and what the driving factors have been behind them. The *why* and not just the *what*.

HOW CAN IT BE DONE BETTER?

The Business Star shown below summarises ten important areas for assessment both in terms of clarifying your **'Here'** reality and defining your **'There'** goals for the future

Each item needs to be properly reviewed and benchmarked before setting the next level goals for the future.

This links in heavily to the recording, reporting, and reviewing of KPIs, but is also based on some other forms of assessment. Examples might include:

➤ **SWOT** *assessment (Strengths, Weaknesses, Opportunities and Threats)*

➤ **PESTLE** *(Political, Economic, Social, Technical, Legal, and Environmental factors)*

➤ *Team performance*

➤ *Market analysis*

This process can be made a little easier by quickly identifying the current business progression stage and defining what the next stage goal is to be:

➤ **Basics Goals** (create a functional business)

➤ **Scalability Goals** (reduce owner reliance, and enable strong growth)

➤ **Independence Goals** (enable the owner to step out from direct involvement)

➤ **Saleability Goals** (prepare the business for sale).

Simply clarifying your current business objective as a whole can help to simplify the goal setting process and ensure that you keep your focus on the right areas at the right time.

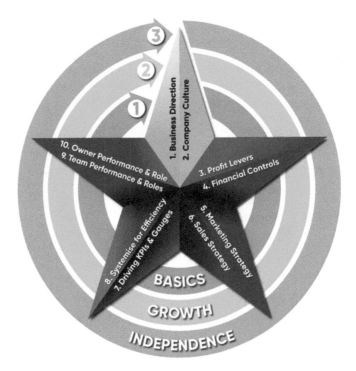

Setting your business goals can be done in a variety of ways. There are the standard business planning documents and a wide variety of spin-offs and alternate approaches used by accountants, consultants, coaches, and gurus.

The advice I'd offer on this would be to consider your own requirements and what you are truly looking to achieve through your planning activity.

1. If it's a case of fulfilling a requirement for someone else (a bank, an investor, etc.) then what do they need to see to make the decision favourably?

2. If it's a case of wanting to push on and progress your business for yourself and your co-directors/shareholders, then perhaps a more 'action focused' plan will be most appropriate.

3. If it's a balance of the two or something else, then do what you feel is right for that!

For the purpose of this book, which is largely focused on achieving business progression and is written for the business owner directly, I'll adopt option 2 from that list and provide some suggestions based on that.

WHAT DO WE MEAN BY AN ACTION PLAN?

Lots of business plans are really summary documents explaining last year's performance and detailing some targeted outcome results for the next period (normally 1–5 years).

Whilst they do contain some assessment of the marketplace, this tends to be more contextual. It's a snapshot of today and the indication of intention for tomorrow more than an action plan.

The key difference is that action plans contain actions and timelines, and normally will also indicate accountability for implementation. The action plan may well also reference the key metrics to be tracked and reported upon to ensure that progress is being made and that the achievements are actually being achieved.

The interesting aspect of this is that action plans need to be living documents. By this I mean that they are not put in a drawer and forgotten about as happens with so many more formal business plans.

How is an action plan created?

I always liken the creation of an action plan to making a Sunday roast.

The first thing is to decide what the meal will comprise. What are the outcomes you are seeking?

In the context of our Business Star, this means a review of what we currently have in place and the results they are bringing (e.g. a discussion on the ten focus areas, a broad appraisal of staging, activities to date, and their metrics/statuses).

Once you have reviewed these, you can set some objectives for each.

For each objective, there will be some supporting goals, and for each goal there will be some supporting actions.

In our metaphor, this might be the equivalent of:

Objective:

Provide a well cooked, nicely prepared, tasty turkey to the dining room table by 1pm.

Goals:

Prepare the turkey for cooking

Cook the bird

Prepare the turkey for the table

Tasks:

Goal: Preparing the turkey for cooking

Tasks: Defrost the turkey and allow it to reach room temperature

Pre-heat the oven

Remove all packaging and giblets

Add the stuffing to the bird

Place the bird into the roasting tray

Add surrounding vegetables and herbs for flavour.

This might sound very obvious, but it's actually nearly always where problems crop up. Making complex things simple is always an art form, and it's pretty common to have to rework a goal a couple of times to identify all the dependencies (tasks that precede the one you think is next).

Most often this comes about when the goal setter forgets that what they are planning on doing is a new activity. This situation often requires some learning, practising, or trial runs before the goal should go live.

It's a mistake to rush in and learn through trial and error in most instances as it leads to errors, rework, and an impact on future goals and timelines. Better to be honest from the outset and start with an assessment of capability before commencing the core goal.

My own mental process for goal setting goes like this:

➤ What do I want to achieve – what's the outcome I want to happen?

➤ What is my current knowledge level on that topic or on the actions required to complete it?

➤ What is my prior experience on executing that task?

➤ Where can I sense-check my understanding, and where can I get support for early implementation if I am not highly skilled or well-practised.

This applies even if the goal is not for my own completion. I just speak to the individuals or team to be involved and get the information needed to set realistic and reasonable expectations.

The resulting goal ends up with this broad framework:

1. Initial learning and research.

2. Supported training and practical trials.

3. Early application and review guidance.

4. Fulfil on remaining activities.

5. Track progress.

6. Review points.

Not every goal includes all steps, but there is a reality that

Capability x Diligence = Outcome

Where:

Capability is a combination of knowledge, mindset, skill, and experience.

Diligence is a combination of planning, discipline, and effort.

When the two aspects of capability and diligence are *both* present with a high rating, the result is amplified substantially.

Think 10 x 10, rather than 2 x 10 or 10 x 2... and you'll get the picture.

Drawing us back one final time to the Dunning Kruger effect spoken about earlier, you can see why I am focusing you heavily onto this approach. Simply put, lots of business owners and their teams apply a lot of effort without the underlying capability being in place first, or they apply a great deal of capability with a limited amount of diligence... and this ends up costing in terms of results more commonly than any would care to admit!

CONNECTING GOALS WITH PERSONAL MOTIVES

Have you ever heard about the little old lady that lifted a car?

Jack Kirby, the author of the *Incredible Hulk* comic books, was apparently inspired to create his now infamous green hero upon a first-hand observation of that very situation. In 1962 he claims to have seen an old lady lift a car that had rolled on top of a baby.

There are many other instances where these extraordinary feats have happened, including one that I can share personally!

THE DAY I THOUGHT WE MIGHT DIE

In a prior career, I was a front line police officer. On one of my night shift duties, I observed a car exit a multi-storey car park in Brighton. As the car left the building and pulled onto the road ahead of me, I noticed that it did not have headlights on. Now whilst the road was well lit due to street lamps and surrounding buildings, I knew that once the vehicle moved away from the town centre, it would become less visible to other road users without its lights on.

As I followed the car along the road, I chose to pull the car over and speak to the driver to advise them to put their headlights on. However, as I turned on the blue lights on top of my police car, the car ahead of me did not stop. In fact, the driver went straight through a red traffic signal and drove off at speed.

After a fairly long pursuit (perhaps five miles) that exceeded a hundred miles per hour at times through a busy city centre setting, the bandit vehicle drove onto the wrong side of the road. At that time, I elected to cancel the pursuit as it had become too dangerous. Unfortunately, my decision did not prevent an accident as just one mile further on, the bandit vehicle struck another vehicle coming the other way.

It was a horrendous crash, with a closing speed that must have been over 100mph. I feared both drivers would have been killed, and as soon as I was able I returned to the location to block the road and attend to the injured parties.

Whilst my colleague went to the bandit vehicle, I ran over to the car of the innocent party, who thankfully appeared unhurt, albeit unconscious. It was at this point that I realised the engine was smoking and there was fuel upon the floor by my feet – obviously from a split fuel tank or line.

As you can imagine, my adrenaline was pumping. I had just had a high speed pursuit, seen a significant collision take place, and expected the worst.

I tugged hard at the driver's door, but it would not open. The metal was bent, and the lock appeared to be engaged. I drew my baton and struck the window, shattering the glass to allow me access. The seatbelt would not release when I reached in, and I drew my penknife to cut the belt and release the driver.

...but despite now manually pulling up the door lock button, the door would still not open, and the other side of the car was completely stoved in. The door was just so bent that it had jammed.

I started to panic as I realised just how dangerous the situation was and that there were now limited options.

It was at this point that I grabbed the door handle in desperation and took hold of the door pillar in my other hand. I pulled as hard as I could, and I heard the shriek of metal as the frame and the door started to inch apart. I put my foot against the pillar and threw all my weight backwards, at which point the door burst open.

I picked up the unconscious driver and I ran with him over my shoulder about forty metres before laying him carefully onto the grass verge.

As I turned around, I saw my colleague chasing the offending driver in the opposite direction and the car I had just been at starting to catch fire. It had been a matter of just a minute or two since the collision, and had I not removed the driver, it could have been a terrible outcome.

That event is scarred in my mind, and I doubt I shall ever forget the fear or the adrenaline surge it delivered.

For those that care, the offending driver was heavily drunk and had made off for that reason. Remarkably, despite his car ending up on its roof with massive damage, he was almost entirely uninjured!

But back to the book principle...

It's remarkable what people can achieve when emotion is involved: when they are committed and they understand the benefits or the consequences for themselves or those they care about.

...which is why I strongly recommend looking deeply at your goals. If you cannot connect them to a motivating impact for you, or someone you care about, then they are less likely to be achieved with energy or enthusiasm.

A good way is to think:

'Who would this help most?'

'How would it make them feel to have that goal completed?'

'What personal impact will it have – now and in the future?'

'Other than me, who will care if this goal is achieved?'

Of course, you should also ask those questions in the context of your own benefits, but one thing I have learned over time is that nearly all of us will let ourselves down in a heartbeat, but when we know the impact is for someone else that we care about, we'll fight lions to get the job done.

This connection between a goal and people is vital. No-one likes to do work for work's sake. There is always a motive. Sometimes personal, sometimes for another... but it's always there.

It's a human trait, and an important one to acknowledge if you want to enhance the performance and effort of both yourself and others.

When it comes to goals, we have to connect the dots – sometimes for ourselves and often for others who we want to assign goals and activities to. This is particularly necessary when giving instructions to colleagues or suppliers. If there is an emotional cost or gain in the completion of the task (immediate or further along), it's vital to communicate this.

I think the best leaders and managers are not necessarily those with the best ideas but those who know how to inspire and energise their team around them.

Just think of Martin Luther King's famous speech 'I have a dream' or of John F Kennedy's famous 'aim to put a man on the moon' project; Steve Jobs' unwavering commitment to the Macintosh computer, Captain Sir Tom Moore's £32 million pound charity walk for the NHS, or the building of the pyramids due to adoration of their god-like pharaohs.

All of these were started with heart and progressed by hand.

Emotion first, logic second. I struggle to think of a single endeavour in human history where great things were achieved by emotionless logical activity alone.

If you want more, better, and faster... engage the heart of those involved; and remember that includes you!

GOAL TIMELINING

One area that most business owners struggle with is time. Never enough of the blasted stuff, and someone lost the recipe for making more!

What this means for business plans and goals is that the reality often diverges from the intention. It's not that you don't want to get the tasks done; it's just that there are too many things to do all of the time.

So how do we overcome that headache?

Well, we can't make more time, which means we need to use it more effectively and to access the time of those around us.

This doesn't come naturally to all business owners.

In fact, a lot of business owners are not great at time management *or* delegation. This is partly because it's in the nature of most entrepreneurs to see a challenge and go straight at it like a bull to a red rag.

...the problem is that, like the bull, it's often not in your best interests to let your attention get drawn.

EFFECTIVE GOALS AND TIME PLANNING

Earlier on in the chapter, you'll have read about splitting goals down into manageable and sequential components. This is important, as when you chunk goals up (particularly to the level of hours or minutes of task), it then become much easier to diary manage.

Two key principles I want to share with you are 'offsetting' and 'instant diary input'.

When it comes to project management (and let's face it, business goals are really just a form of project), there are many excellent pieces of software available to help.

Whether it's a Kanban board, list managers, or full-on project management software, they all share the benefits of both visibility and tracing.

OFFSETTING

If you've ever seen a one-man-band play, you'll understand what a rare skill they possess: the ability to handle multiple tasks simultaneously without missing a beat is extraordinary!

In most cases, musicians best play one instrument at a time. Not just through skill and focus, but also the reality that they only have one mouth, two hands (and for the drummers, two feet) to involve. There is a limitation to what they can realistically undertake at once.

The same is true for business owners. If you need to involve an orchestra to help out, that is much better than trying to play 70 instruments yourself... all at the same time!

Option one, therefore, is resourcing and using your team and others to allow simultaneous goals to run.

Option two (for most a reality due to limited funds and the availability of skilled and trusted workmates) is 'offsetting'.

Offsetting is simply the method by which you assess the priorities and potential for overlapping of goals.

Prioritisation can be made on a variety of factors, but overlapping is solely down to your own capability, or the capability of your team, to complete multiple tasks during the same short timeframe (e.g. today or this week).

The breakdown of goals talked about earlier in terms of time is one thing; the other is simply the ability to split your focus and maintain effectiveness. Personally, I have never been much good at doing more than one complex and brain intensive task at a time... I suspect the same is true for you – whether you'll admit it or not!

Offsetting involves the balancing of time, focus, and resource in a way that allows rapid and proper progression against intended tasks and goals.

Depending on the capability, diligence, and realism of the team, this may result in one, two, or more goals being worked on at the same time... there isn't a right answer for all situations, but those are the factors to consider.

One method of displaying these goals is a Gantt chart.

This shows the overlap and offset of different tasks in a visual manner, either for one or multiple goals.

YOUR GOALS	Week 1	Week 2	Week 3	Week 4	Week 5	Week 6	Week 7	Week 8
Goal 1 SMART format	Task 1 e.g. learning	Task 2 e.g. Instruction	Task 3 activity	Task 4 review	Task 5 finalise	Task 6 finalise		
Accountability – who	John	John	Mary	John/Mary	Steve	John		
Tracking measure (if relevant)				KPI required				
Goal 2 SMART format				Task 1 e.g. learning	Task 2 e.g. activity	Task 3 review		
Accountability – who				Andy	Andy	Andy/John		
Tracking measure (if relevant)						KPI required		
Goal 3 SMART format							Task 1 e.g. activity	Task 2 review
Accountability – who							John	John/Andy
Tracking measure (if relevant)								KPI required

Personally, I like this format as whilst very simple, it is also very easy to use and snapshot progress against, particularly when coupled with a RAG (red, amber, green) mark-up.

Green indicates completed, red indicates behind schedule, and yellow indicates the task is still to come but not behind or ahead.

SIMPLE, BUT EFFECTIVE

In a 'real' example, there would be more detail included in the relevant boxes (sufficient that the goal cannot be misinterpreted, and the tasks are clear and do not allow the person responsible to 'wriggle out' from their commitments). The KPI would also be described by name and likely have a target metric or parameter level stated.

In the version above, it has been set over an eight week period. Generally, I use these types of forms for quarterly action planning in my own business and with clients, but they can be scaled to any size or duration within reason.

Where your business is involved in larger-scale projects or perhaps has overlapping projects (e.g. construction companies, software development businesses), then I would strongly recommend seeking out and utilising technological solutions designed for that purpose. Lots are based on PRINCE2 or Agile methodologies specific to given industries.

The examples I provide here are intended for less operational and more broad business or personal goal planning and tracking purposes.

Again, there are lots of apps and software solutions for those too – it is the principles of this approach I want you to focus upon for now.

The exact how, is up to you!

INSTANT DIARY INPUT

When using software (project management, Customer Relationship Management or CRM software etc.), often tasks and diary entries will go hand in hand automatically, but where they don't, this human habit is a great one to adopt.

It's simple: as soon as you have agreed and committed to tasks in a plan, assign the time and the tasks immediately into your diary. Decide on when you will get those actions done.

This means that you won't reach that week and then have to try and 'create time' in your already stacked diary. At worst you may need to adjust when you complete these tasks a little within that week, but the unwritten rule is that short of a true crisis, these strategic, longer term goal actions are not moved out from that week.

This might seem an easy discipline, but I promise you it takes commitment.

I have lost count of the times where I or my clients have tried to justify why we need to defer the strategic goal for today's challenge. It's a dangerous behaviour to adopt too often as the strategic will never get done, and the challenges never stop. There is nearly always something 'urgent' for today but also something 'important' for your future... balancing the two takes iron self-discipline and a separation of your duties as a business owner from the duties of other roles in your business.

One way of managing this internal conflict of interests is to ring-fence time in your diary every week or every month that is exclusively for strategic business goals and thinking (i.e. **ON** the business time)

A non-negotiable commitment to business improvement and progression!

Chapter 4 – Reflection and Exercise

Please mark the **type** of goals that now need to be set for each area of The Business Star. This takes account of the situation **NOW** and the **NEXT** step change you want to happen.

	Basics	Scalability	Independence
Business Direction	❏	❏	❏
Business Culture	❏	❏	❏
Profit Levers	❏	❏	❏
Financial Control	❏	❏	❏
Marketing Strategy	❏	❏	❏
Sales Strategy	❏	❏	❏
KPIs and Gauges	❏	❏	❏
Business Systems	❏	❏	❏
Team Performance/Role	❏	❏	❏
Owner Performance/Role	❏	❏	❏

Chapter 5

BUSINESS CULTURE

So far, we have spoken of the direction of the company in terms of progression stages and action planning, but great companies are founded upon more than a desire for profit.

Of course profit is important, even core to a business, but it shouldn't be the sole reason for its existence. If it is, then the focus of the company becomes too insular – focused exclusively on the benefit of the shareholders.

Above the profit goal, there needs to be a unifying theme – a guiding light to drive the actions, ethics, and behaviours of those involved.

The purpose statement is what provides this. It explains the 'why' behind the 'what'.

When defined effectively, a purpose statement acts as a directional beacon to draw the company onwards. A 'North Star', if you like.

In my business coaching practice, the normal starting point in working with a new client is called the 'North Star Meeting' for this reason. The intention is to confirm the purpose of their business, agree the purpose of our work together, and establish how far along the journey they are now, before confirming where we are going to travel together.

Within your business, the purpose statement should deliver a similar outcome for your employees, suppliers, team, and other interested parties. When they have read it, they should be able to clearly see what it is that you stand for and how your business relates to that.

As an example of this, when I first started coaching I did not have a purpose statement. This was partly because I had joined a franchise that had its own vision and values to which I was aligned, but more because I simply hadn't given it enough thought.

Now, almost 12 years later and having worked with several hundred different businesses and owners, I am clearer on what my purpose is.

I have now documented this and broadened it to encompass my business as a whole rather than myself as an individual.

> **'At UK Growth Coach, our purpose is to simplify the business of business for company owners, and to be the positive catalyst that drives meaningful personal change, business growth, and life results.**
>
> **The outcome of our work will be fewer company failures and more business successes. It will cause greater enjoyment and happiness for the owners, their teams, their clients, and others they influence.'**

As the head of my company, this purpose fires me up. It tells me why what I do is important and why I should get up in the morning and do my best.

It gets my energy up, and when I have a bad day (as we all do), I read it to myself to remind myself that what my team and I do has real, valuable meaning and reason behind it.

Having talked this purpose statement through with a number of clients and others who work with my business, I have seen the shift in their perception of myself as an individual as well as the way they view my company.

The purpose statement is more than just a corporate headline or PR (Public Relations) exercise. It's there to stir the blood and fire the senses.

It should inspire and engage others who share a desire to see those results in their world or in themselves, or want to be part of something with that ambition.

In other words, it means something, and it's a truly personal driver.

My question is this: 'If I read the purpose statement for your business, would I get an ounce of the same emotional impact?'

If so, that's great.

If you aren't sure, then have a tweak.

But if you know for sure that the answer is 'no', then do something about it before you get too far into the detail of tasks and timings. You have to engage the hearts as much as the minds if your business is going to fly!

The strange thing about this topic is that purpose drives culture, and that a business with strong purpose and strong culture is likely (providing the core business model is also strong) to be more profitable.

As with my example of the old lady lifting the car off the baby, inspired and passionate people who have a reason for doing their work well just put more effort and diligence in. It's that straightforward. Emotional engagement and value alignment *really* matter in creating successful companies.

CREATING A CLEAR SET OF VALUES AND GETTING EVERYONE ALIGNED

Purpose statements say, 'Beyond profit, **this** is why we exist.'

Company values are more about saying, 'This is what we stand for.'

The values are the basis for displayed attitude and behaviour within the company. They define the type of people the business wants to present.

This is normally communicated in two formats:

Service values are communicated to prospects, customers, and partners to explain what the company considers as being important to those groups and the way they want to be perceived. These are often heavily related to the experience they want to deliver – e.g. honesty, respect for your time, treat your home as our own, value for money, and so on.

Team values are more to do with the attitudes and behaviour of the personnel that represent the company and how they operate across the business (beyond the customer-facing aspects).

When defined well, these can also act as a baseline for the recruitment of new team members. They lead to assessments that go beyond technical capability or academic qualifications, by using a behavioural framework.

This can be amazingly helpful as it is not always the most academic that make the best colleagues!

Examples of team values might be: organised, careful, truthful, committed to personal learning, focused on solutions not problems, respectful, and so on.

DEVELOPING VALUES INTO BEHAVIOURS THAT GO BEYOND THE EXPECTED

These values can become the basis of 'Team-ship rules' – a concept I learned from Sir Clive Woodward (the English rugby coach who took his team to 2003 World Cup victory and who was heavily involved in the organisation of Team GB for the Beijing Olympics).

Team-ship rules are agreed standards of behaviour that the team commit to that demonstrate their values in a given setting. An example might be where 'cleanliness' is a value in a hospital setting. Whilst the health and safety advice may create a minimum standard, a team-ship rule would push the level of care and attention to that aspect higher. It is where a team decides that 'good enough' isn't, and that a higher standard needs to be demonstrated.

Eric Jerome Dickey (in his book Sleeping with Strangers) wrote that 'Early is on time, on time is late, and late is unacceptable.' This quote is often used to talk about team management for meetings and other appointments, and it's a good example of the type of thinking that team-ship and team values can bring. When agreed upon as a team-ship rule, that quote would make it 'psychologically uncomfortable' for a colleague to be late to a meeting within that team.

Other notable examples relate to personal knowledge (for taxi drivers in London), hygiene (for water bottle management of the Olympic team in Beijing), and appearance (for military parades and inspections).

I have seen this type of principle in use in a number of businesses and can attest to it being effective and also leading to a sense of team pride in how members act and behave towards one another and others affected by their 'higher standards'.

One key point to note here is the need for involvement of the *whole* team in the setting of these team-ship rules. These *higher than expected* standards need to be agreed to by *all* members of that group and should not be adopted otherwise (in most instances). They become expected not because of a contract of employment but because a team is inspired to perform to their best, not their average.

This is very different to regular performance standards, which of course can be set, monitored, and managed if needed. There is no requirement for all team members to agree to the setting of those – although I'd always recommend clear discussion to ensure understanding and clarity and avoid frustration either way around.

The ethos of team-ship rules is that they are driven and inspired by the team's desire to perform better.

It takes a particular style of leadership and management to engage this type of team thinking and commitment, but when it's achieved, these teams perform like no others.

As with all other forms of performance standard, these need to be set, be encouraged, be tracked, and have some accountability and recognition management.

So often the achievement and maintenance of these high standards is through gratitude and appreciation. Remember, the donkey only moves just fast enough to avoid the stick but will run as hard as they can to win a carrot!

Chapter 5 – Reflection and Exercise

Our business purpose statement is:

....

....

....

....

Our top three company service values are:

1. ....

This means:

....

....

2. ....

This means:

....

....

3. ....

This means:

....

....

Chapter 6

THE NINE PROFIT LEVERS

Whilst purpose is vital, so too is profit.

I've yet to see someone cashing in their end of month purpose to pay the bills.

When speaking with business owners, I often ask what they want to achieve.

Many will start by saying that they want more time, better marketing, a more productive team, etcetera.

However, when I ask them what they want as an outcome for all of their hard work, they almost universally say they want a good income, a healthy pension, security, and freedom of choice in life.

Now to achieve the results wanted in the second list, you need a healthy business profit.

The first list is much more about overcoming headaches that are either a function of poor profit or indicate a poor return on hours invested.

So what drives up profit?

I'll give you a heads up: it isn't just one element, and it *does* vary a bit from company to company!

However, there are nine relatively consistent levers that exist to boost business profitability. These are outlined in the diagram on the next page.

The Nine Profit Levers model

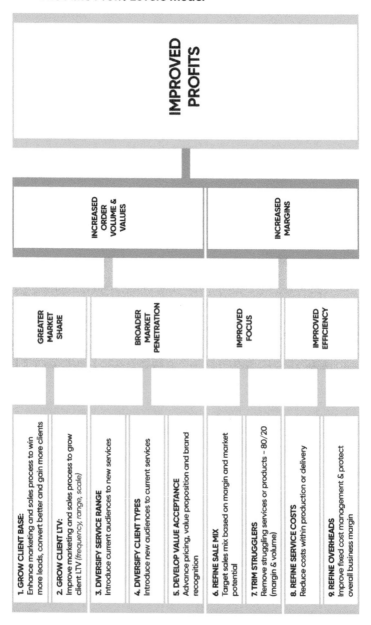

IMPROVED PROFITS

INCREASED ORDER VOLUME & VALUES

INCREASED MARGINS

GREATER MARKET SHARE

BROADER MARKET PENETRATION

IMPROVED FOCUS

IMPROVED EFFICIENCY

1. GROW CLIENT BASE:
Enhance marketing and sales process to win more leads, convert better and gain more clients

2. GROW CLIENT LTV:
Improve marketing and sales process to grow client LTV (frequency, range, scale)

3. DIVERSIFY SERVICE RANGE
Introduce current audiences to new services

4. DIVERSIFY CLIENT TYPES
Introduce new audiences to current services

5. DEVELOP VALUE ACCEPTANCE
Advance pricing, value proposition and brand recognition

6. REFINE SALE MIX
Target sales mix based on margin and market potential

7. TRIM STRUGGLERS
Remove struggling services or products – 80/20 (margin & volume)

8. REFINE SERVICE COSTS
Reduce costs within production or delivery

9. REFINE OVERHEADS
Improve fixed cost management & protect overall business margin

Now, it's important to note that each of the nine levers will have an impact on the Driving KPIs (which will be explored in more detail later in this book).

For now, I am not looking at the associated measures but more at the strategy of using the levers on the front end of a business.

Let's take each in turn:

1. Building your client base

This is perhaps the most obvious way to increase profit, and it is certainly the most common default for business owners who have growth in mind. 'If we want more profit, let's get more customers.'

It isn't, however, always the most efficient approach.

We'll be looking at sales and marketing strategy in the next few chapters, so I'll just leave that thought floating for the time being.

2. Growing your customer lifetime value
(also known as client lifetime value)

Customer lifetime value is where the serious profit lies for many businesses – especially those that either make a loss, break-even, or make only a minimal profit on the first transaction.

This may be due to the cost of setting up/starting with a new customer or because of the cost of acquisition (how much it costs you in marketing and sales time/investment).

Whatever the reason, and even if you are profitable on the first sale, it is highly likely that during your customer's lifetime, there will be the chance for secondary sales.

Whilst on the first occasion there may well have been a substantial investment to 'buy that customer' or to 'onboard' them, the likelihood is that further sales will come if the initial experience is positive and the relationship is nurtured forward.

If the company offers a naturally recurring service such as annual tax returns from an accountant, that's easy. If it is a case of cross-selling or introducing a secondary service, then it may take a little more graft.

The key here is to have a strategy/set of strategies for ongoing communication with your customers.

You need to maintain an up-to-date knowledge of their situation and needs, and to ensure that you maintain a recognised and valued service relationship.

Look after them, show that you care, work the system, and keep the orders coming!

3. DIVERSIFYING YOUR SERVICE RANGE

It's quite common for us to answer questions that clients express outwardly, but not to answer the silent passive ones.

By this, I mean that when we serve clients, we get into the habit of only exploring their apparent needs and those for which we *currently* provide a service or solution.

However, when we are looking to grow our profit, it's worth asking, 'What else do my clients have a need for, and perhaps even buy at a similar time to when they buy from us?'

An example of this might be a customer purchasing a new will when having just bought a new home.

Yet the lawyer who managed the conveyancing may potentially miss this obvious cross-sell opportunity if they haven't clicked on the timing and relevance.

At the same time, it's highly likely that some insurances will be reviewed, and perhaps that adds in another opportunity. After all, as a customer, it's often easier to deal with one supplier who can solve a host of requirements than to deal with lots of individual suppliers for each.

Taking a detailed look at your core customers and identifying where additional needs can be met by your business can open up a wide range of opportunities for additional profit.

4. Diversifying client types

It is also worth considering the alternate approach of keeping the same service mix but broadening the audiences that you provide those services to.

This involves researching who else (beyond the current client base) has a need for the services and solutions that you provide. In many cases, this isn't actually as difficult as it might seem.

Most people assume that this 'new audience' is someone as yet unidentified, but more often it's the case that it is an already identified audience that has not yet been accessed at all or in a meaningful volume.

The easiest way to start is to run an audit of the clients that you have been serving to date. Identify the current mix and compare it against the target audiences that you had in mind when you created the services or the initial marketing plan.

Where there are gaps between intention and reality, there is opportunity, and where you identify peaks in a particular audience, you may also be recognising the potential to sell a product or service to a high volume and engaged niche sector (e.g. if you were in the fitness industry, you might discover that you could provide a specialist fitness service specifically for rehabilitation of injured sportspeople, and had just not realised that this is a core audience for you).

Diversifying the client types can also, obviously involve assessing new potential markets that you have *not* yet accessed. This might be simply a new audience type, or may be down to enhanced geographic range (e.g. a new warehouse and delivery team), change in methodology (e.g. a shift from traditional face-to-face services to online provision), or something else.

Importance of balancing risk and strategic choices

One very important principle to raise at this stage is the **Ansoff Matrix**. This is a basic marketing model commonly taught to marketers but not actually very well-known in the broader business owner community. The principle is based upon a classic four square model that has two main axes.

The X axis relates to products, and the Y axis relates to markets. There are only two criteria for each axis: either existing or new.

Reference: Ansoff, H. I. (1957). Strategies for Diversification. *Harvard Business Review.* (Vol. 35 Issue 5, Sep/Oct). p113-124.

There are a few vital points to note in this diagram for making informed business decisions.

Obviously, as with all principles, there will be exceptions, but in the main it works!

Here is what you need to know...

The first point is that marketing your known products and services to an already established and known market is the safest strategy. The customers are already familiar with the existence and experience of those services, and the means of communicating the value proposition and winning the orders is already well proven. The risk factor for this type of marketing is rated as 1.

NEW TO KNOWN
Risk Factor = 4

The next point is that marketing new products or services, but to a known and existing client market is the next tier of risk. It comes in at a rating of 4 (nominally viewed as four times less likely to succeed that 'known to known'). Whilst not ideal, the reality is that most businesses do need to broaden their approach from time to time.

KNOWN TO NEW
Risk Factor = 4

Similarly, marketing existing products and services to new markets is at the same risk level (4). It is fairly common for companies to elect to 'trial' the promotion of an existing service or product to a new marketplace. This happens every time a business chooses to expand into a new country for example. Again, the risk factor is four times higher than known to known, but it is not extreme or unnecessary in most instances.

NEW TO NEW
Risk Factor = 14

Finally, we come to new services/products being presented to new markets.

This carries a risk factor of 14 and represents the highest risk form of marketing. It also represents every brand-new company's situation and in part explains why the failure rate of new companies is so high. Convincing new contacts to buy a new offering for the very first time is the hardest combination of all.

I am choosing to explain this model here as it is an important aspect for your business and marketing strategy. The general advice would be to stick to familiar and proven ground where you can. If you need to diversify, then choose one axis, not both... unless you can't.

This is guidance not a hard and fast rule.

In business, there is always risk, and many companies have chosen to launch new products to new markets and have done so very successfully indeed, but the odds were not with them at the outset. The safe bet would not have been there.

The key point I am making is that it is better to take an informed risk than a blind one.

If you are moving into new sectors, particularly if you are going into the high risk section of the Anshoff Matrix, the guidance I would always give would be to do your homework first.

Stack the deck in your favour by completing some thorough market research, and gather the evidence to back up your hopes and dreams before you commit the business security or your life savings to that direction.

Be pragmatic, and if you still feel brave with all the data to hand, then it's your call, and I wish you all the best with it!

5. DEVELOP VALUE ACCEPTANCE

Getting full value (or not) for your service or your product can make or break a business. It's a simple case of mathematics and is normally considered when considering discounts or price increases. The grid below makes this point nicely.

For clarity, the sales price minus the cost of sales equals the gross profit.

	STARTING VALUES	-10% PRICE DISCOUNT	+10% PRICE INCREASE
SALES PRICE	£100	£90	£110
COST OF SALES	£70	£70	£70
GROSS PROFIT	£30	£20	£40

ALLOWS FOR UP TO -25% SALES DECREASE

REQUIRES +50% SALES

Here you can see the *true* impact of either applying a 10% discount or a 10% price increase.

For both scenarios, the cost of sales remains the same, but the impact on sales value carries directly through to the resulting gross profit. *(note: assumes CoS is 100% variable)*

In the case of the 10% price discount, this equates to a requirement for **+50%** in sales volume, in order to achieve the same profit.

(i.e. 150% x £20 = £30)

In the case of the 10% price increase, the business could see a 25% fall in sales volume and not actually experience a loss in gross profit.

(i.e. 75% of £40 is £10, and £40 – £10 = £30)

There are obviously other factors to consider, but the key aspect to be fully aware of is that the impact on the business profitability is substantially higher than the percentage increase/discount applied to the sale price.

This is very clear when displayed in this format but not always well considered by business owners or their teams when seeking to plug a 'gap in sales'. Sales teams are often very keen on promotions that make their job easier (e.g. a discount makes it easier for them to sell, and unless their commission is tied to profitability, they may be more motivated by personal benefit than benefit to the business).

In many cases, it is true that a customer may be more motivated to buy when a price has been lowered, but the key question is whether the business is sufficiently confident about the intended uplift in volume being achieved.

When there is any confusion about the level of change required, this can lead to a poor strategic decision being made. For example, if the business owner mistakenly believed that they just needed to achieve more than a 10% sales volume increase to offset the impact of a 10% sales value discount in the example above, that could be a very serious misjudgement indeed!

Overleaf are a pair of grids that will make this a bit easier for you:

Discount Matrix

% Price Reduction	Current Gross Profit %							
	10	15	20	25	30	35	40	50
	Percentage that sales must increase to maintain total gross profit							
2.0	25	15	11	9	7	6	5	4
3.0	43	25	18	14	11	9	8	6
4.0	67	36	25	19	15	13	11	9
5.0	100	50	22	25	20	17	14	11
10.0		200	100	67	50	40	33	25
15.0			300	150	100	75	60	43

Price Rise Matrix

% Price Reduction	Current Gross Profit %							
	10	15	20	25	30	35	40	50
	Percentage that sales can fall before total gross profit reduces							
2.0	17	12	9	7	6	5	5	4
3.0	23	17	13	11	9	8	7	6
4.0	29	21	17	14	12	10	9	7
5.0	33	25	20	17	14	12	11	9
10.0	50	40	33	29	25	22	20	17
15.0	60	50	43	37	33	30	27	23

In each case the left hand column shows the discount or increase intended percentage.

The current gross profit for the initial pricing is important as that sets the benchmark against which you are looking to identify the change impact.

The columns beneath the relevant initial gross profit number, when cross-referenced with the intended adjustment, will give you a percentage of change impact.

As an example, if you take the 30% gross profit we used for our initial example, and apply the 10% discount, you can see that the number it references is 50. This 50 is telling you that you would need an uplift in sales volume of 50% to achieve the same profit.

Likewise, for the 10% price increase, on the 30% initial gross margin, you can see the cross-referencing indicates the number 25. This is telling you that you could tolerate a 25% reduction in sales volume as a result of applying that price increase and not be worse off in terms of direct gross profit.

I have always found these grids to be very beneficial for my own companies but also when coaching clients. I hope they create a bit of an 'aha' moment for you and become a useful reference when considering the pricing of your service or product.

Back to value achievement...

The reason for sharing those insights is simple – you will be more tempted (I hope) to defend the full value pricing for your services and products when you can clearly see the impact of failing to do so.

Whilst the tactics of 'sell it cheap' and 'stack it high' are valid in certain settings, most smaller businesses that are competing on a local level don't have the ability to sell for the lowest prices and still make a profit.

They also are unlikely to have sufficient profit generated from other areas of the company to tolerate a loss leader strategy for an extended period... better to ensure you maximise the profit on the sales you do make than to make a minimum in the hope of higher volume.

To do so means identifying the right pricing for the right service or product, and often this is a case of research, as well as testing and measuring.

I once heard a coach describe pricing as being an elastic band. You can stretch it out gently until it snaps. The snap is when you are consistently getting 'No, it's too expensive' as the overriding objection, and you need to be sure that this isn't just down to being poor at communicating the value proposition!

The value proposition and customer profile

Dr Alexander Osterwalder is a Swiss business theorist, author, speaker, and consultant. I have researched a number of concepts he has developed, and particularly like the 'Value Proposition Canvas' he has defined.

It is a really useful tool for ensuring the fit between a product or service and the market.

In broad terms, it is based on two foundation blocks: the customer profile and the value proposition.

The customer profile is based on three elements:

1. **The gains.** These are the benefits that the customer is hoping to receive, and can be a balance of expectation and wishes.

2. **The pains.** These are the frustrations, irritations, and other negative facets that a customer experiences either whilst completing a 'job' or their expectation in completing a future one.

3. **Customer 'jobs'.** In this setting, customer jobs are described as being functional, social, or emotional tasks. They are any actions that a customer needs to complete, issues they are trying to resolve, or needs they wish to meet.

In essence, these three elements combine to form a profile that is the basis from which a customer avatar can be built. For this reason, it is necessary to build a customer profile for each audience you wish to market to or influence. Each will have distinct jobs they wish to complete, gains they wish to benefit from, and pains they wish to diminish.

The value proposition

The value proposition is effectively the second puzzle piece that neatly connects with the first half created by the customer profile When the proposition is well considered and a match is present for each of the three components, then a sale is highly likely to take place.

The value proposition is therefore, as you may well imagine, also based upon three related components.

These are:

1. **Gain Creators.** These are 'hows'. How the solution creates customer beneficial outcomes and how it goes above and beyond a baseline expectation. To achieve maximum value, you have to aim for 'beyond satisfaction' and step into the realm of 'delivering on their wishes as well as their expectations'.

2. **Pain Relievers.** These are also 'hows'. How your proposed solution reduces frustrations, pains, annoyances, and irritations… and also how the customer will feel after they have gone – helping the client visualise, and emotionally connect with the release of negativity!

3. **Products and Services.** These are the solutions you can present that package up the gain creators and the pain relievers. Most businesses start by talking about these, but in reality the customers don't care about them until they know what they can offer in terms of gain achievement or pain removal.

Take a look at the image on the next page to see how this all lines up…

6. REFINE THE SALES MIX

Lots of businesses simply report their turnover and profit as a summary. One figure for total sales, one for all costs of sale, one for company gross profit, then all overheads as one number, and finally an EBITDA (Earnings before interest, tax, depreciation or amortisation) **or** a net profit number.

It's easy that way, and for many SMEs (Small to Medium Enterprises) it is the preferred method for bookkeepers or 'compliance accountants'. It's not wrong, but it isn't as helpful as it could be.

Understanding where your business profit centres are is vital to efficiency, and when you have restrictions on output (perhaps due to space limitations at a factory site, or as a small consultancy it may be due to a limited number of billable hours), it can be really helpful to understand where you are making profit most effectively.

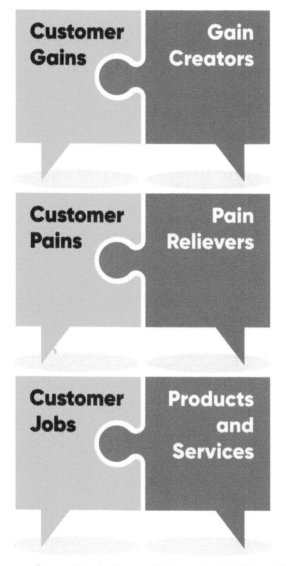

Reference: Osterwalder, A., Pigneur, Y., Bernarda, G., Smith, A. (2014) *Value Proposition Design: How to Create Products and Services Customers Want.* John Wiley & Sons.

Now, it's important for me to point out that what I am going to show you here is the simple version. There are other aspects which do matter and should be considered before you make any drastic changes, but the maths doesn't lie...

Below are three different scenarios.

Scenario 1 is for a business that did not have any particular focus on the different products or services it was selling. It simply sold what it could and ended up 'somewhere' as a result.

The summary shows three different streams of income, and it also shows the margin that each achieves.

In the example, all three elements achieve the same level of turnover, but they each produce a different level of profit thanks to the differences in margins.

The resulting gross profit for the company is £150,000 when all three are added together.

Scenario 1	Starting Sales Mix		
	Product or Service 1	Product or Service 2	Product of Service 3
Sales Turnover Achieved	£100,000	£100,000	£100,000
Total Turnover	£300,000		
Gross Margin	80%	50%	20%
Gross Profit	£80,000	£50,000	£20,000
Resulting Combined Gross Profit	£150,000		

Scenario 2 shows how that company might perform the following year, as it continues to be reactive to existing habits rather than pro-active towards an intentional sales strategy.

In this example, the sales turnover for revenue streams 1 and 3 (i.e. the high and low margin elements) have shifted in ratio.

The impact is that whilst the turnover for the company overall has remained static year-on-year (it is still £300,000 annually), the gross profit has reduced substantially (dropping from £150,000 to £120,000).

This was not a targeted result, and the reason behind the change is only highly visible because we have separated out the data to show the different revenue (and profit) streams. This is showing how important that level of reporting is in truly understanding your business.

Scenario 2	Potential of No Sales Mix Focus		
	Product or Service 1	Product or Service 2	Product of Service 3
Sales Turnover Achieved	£50,000	£100,000	£150,000
Total Turnover	£300,000		
Gross Margin	80%	50%	20%
Gross Profit	£40,000	**£50,000**	£30,000
Resulting Combined Gross Profit	Down to	£120,000	

Scenario 3 shows what might have happened in a parallel world, had the business in scenario 1 stopped for a moment to consider its plan for the following year.

In this example, they identified that demand for their services was relatively equal and that if they refocused their marketing and sales efforts, they should be able to positively steer prospects and customers towards the services and products that yielded higher margin for the business.

Scenario 3	Potential of Positive Sales Mix Focus		
	Product or Service 1	Product or Service 2	Product of Service 3
Sales Turnover Achieved	£150,000	£100,000	£50,000
Total Turnover	£300,000		
Gross Margin	80%	50%	20%
Gross Profit	£120,000	**£50,000**	£10,000
Resulting Combined Gross Profit	Up to	£180,000	

Now, to be clear, the margin in this instance was not a function of pricing alone. The business was achieving high margins on product/service 1 because they had won a really good deal with a supplier of raw materials, and this meant that the costs to them were low for that particular line. It wasn't a case of just selling higher value items or in any way 'abusing' customers... it was simply business opportunity, and the recognition of it!

By selling a higher proportion of the higher margin service/product line, the business was able to make a higher overall gross profit, *despite* having some limitations on production output. Therefore, the same turnover (£300,000) was able to yield a better profit (£180,000) solely by shifting the sales mix.

Obviously, if you are able to shift the mix favourably *and* scale up the volume, it has a magnified effect for your company!

7. TRIM THE STRUGGLERS

In nearly all businesses, there are 'strugglers'.

These are the products that sit on the shelf for longer than they should, the clients who pay late or always quibble over price, the prospects who ask for quote after quote but never place a real or substantial order, the staff members who are stuck in slow gear, and the services that eat up time or resource but don't actually make much profit after all is said and done.

They are the wasted effort and the non-starters, and it's easy to tolerate them as a part of your business just through habit or inaction. The reality is that these elements of your company are using up your focus, time, money, or energy in a non-productive way.

By 'trimming these strugglers' out, you'll put yourself and your business in a position to move forward more positively, more swiftly, more efficiently, and more enjoyably! Oh, and almost universally, you'll be spending less on the administration of the related tasks, and that makes it more profitable too!

Often, you'll discover the struggling services and products through the revenue stream separation process above, the team members through performance reviews, and the wasteful prospects and customers by either a more robust qualification process or a 'grading' exercise. More on some of these points later!

8. Refine service costs

When you are looking to improve your gross profit, there are two main factors that can affect that:

1. The sales value achieved (which we have just covered in the previous section).

2. The costs to your business of providing that product or service.

Here we are looking at item number 2, and there are a few items to consider that can play into the outcomes you achieve:

➤ Direct costs

➤ Clarity on requirement versus preference

➤ Supplier relationships

➤ Internal inefficiencies in delivery, provision, and other human elements

➤ Collateral damages!

Direct costs are fairly obvious and include such things as cost of raw materials, production processes, and so on. Generally speaking, this is a case of keeping an eye on each line item and monitoring for changes.

It is very common for supply costs to move, and unless you are watching for this actively, it can be easy to find that the costs to you have risen and have not been identified in time to reflect those adjustments in sales pricing or to renegotiate and challenge with the suppliers.

Nowadays there are some very good systems in terms of procurement and accounting that allow for direct tracking of these costs and that flag any alterations.

When negotiating with your suppliers, it can also be highly beneficial to look at strategies such as fixing rates or considering bulk orders for discounts if cashflow and the product storage lifespan will suit.

For more service-based businesses, there may be other costs such as time travelling to or from meetings, over-run on meetings, and so forth that unless measured, will not show up easily in the tracking of direct costs. They can, however, have a dramatic impact on profit per hour, and, as a second impact, the capacity for taking on further clients will be limited sooner than would otherwise be necessary. Other factors can include using sub-contractors at different pay rates or work rates.

The clarity on requirement versus preference is an interesting one. Whilst coaching many business owners over time, there have been occasions when reviewing costs that a personal preference is causing a profit margin to be reduced unnecessarily.

One example of this was a business owner continuing to use a supplier for print materials purely based on a personal friendship that was external to the business. The supplier was aware of that relationship lever and was using it to their advantage, and thus charging a fair amount higher than other similar suppliers in the marketplace. When this was highlighted, and a discussion held over the impact of the friendship on the profitability of the company, it was easy for the business owner to re-approach that supplier and negotiate a better rate. It's not uncommon for business owners to build friendships with their suppliers and for those suppliers to 'take advantage' of that relationship.

It's natural, and there isn't anything sordid in that, but ultimately it is a game of business not a game of friendship. Whilst it's nice to have a friend, I also demand that my business friends are competitive in their dealings, or they will have to accept that we'll still be friends, but they may not still be my supplier!

This took me a while to realise as a business owner, in the same way as it's important to realise that whilst you can have friendships with your staff, there is also likely to be a conflict of interests that has to be managed in a business-manner from time to time.

Supplier relationships can have an effect in the way mentioned above (i.e. the abuse of friendship), but more often the issues arise due to negative relationships. If you don't maintain a positive, professional, and amiable relationship with suppliers, you almost certainly will not get the best deals available.

Elements such as trust and transparency, and the simplicity of dealing with you, can make a real difference to the costs, flexibility, and attitude of a supplier. As a general rule of thumb, from a cashflow perspective I advise clients to pay suppliers on the last day of the agreed terms, but to do that every single time without fail. This consistency is important, as suppliers are generally happy as the payment is within terms and therefore to their expectation. If it is abused or inconsistent (particularly late and inconsistent) that can really strain a relationship.

One might argue, therefore, 'Isn't it worth me paying early then to win a bit of positivity?'

It's a fair question, and if you are going to go down that route, there are two points to query. First, is the impact on your business cashflow achievable without causing any needless challenges on that front? Second, what are you gaining? Be clear on what your advantage will be, and go and negotiate it properly and record the agreement properly. If you will promise to pay on day 7 rather than day 30, and therefore will be boosting your supplier's cashflow whilst simultaneously diminishing your own, what are you 'buying' with that arrangement? Is it a faster delivery schedule, a better cost rate, or something else? As with all other forms of business agreement, you need to clarify, confirm, and record what the commitments are, both from yourself and from the other party – i.e. you will do this for me, and in exchange, I will do this for you. This isn't a matter of suggested behaviour but a solid and documented promise between both parties. This mindset is important as once those agreements have been made, it is often the ability to openly challenge the integrity of that party that gets the situation back on track fast... far faster and more simply than any legal process.

Internal inefficiencies in delivery, provision, and other human elements

As with all processes that involve humans, there will be inefficiencies and inconsistencies. Some, such as the tracking of time for given tasks, are quite easy to identify and deal with, but others are tougher to weed out and optimise.

This is particularly challenging for tasks that are either completed in an inconsistent manner and/or undertaken less frequently. In many cases, those undertaking these tasks will justify variation by saying, 'Oh, these are always unique,' whereas the truth of the matter is that they mean, 'These aren't very common, and I don't want to go to the effort of systemising.'

In almost all situations where a task is going to be repeated several times, a system would aid efficiency and consistency.

Of course, whilst a fair consideration of the cost of systemisation versus the benefit it brings is relevant, it shouldn't be the basis of a lazy excuse!

Only when a system has been laid out, followed, and assessed can a business really look to optimise an output. If the elements are done differently each time, then the overall result may change, and it's nigh on impossible to identify the aspect that was the cause. The measure under review might be fuel use, wastage, staff time use, or some other element, but you need to be systematic and precise in what you want to refine if you are to achieve the greatest success in minimising costs and maximising efficiencies.

One world that demonstrates this focus on excellence and efficiency is Formula One racing, where team members will systemise, practice, trial, and refine a working approach over and over again. In that context, the objective is most often a time gain rather than a cost reduction, but the approach is still relevant. If you want to deliver the ultimate, it's rarely achieved through the first system applied.

9. REFINE OVERHEADS

Whilst the gross margin and resulting gross profit are certainly very important focus points when looking to drive up the overall net profit for a company, these are one of two main cost control foci.

The second is to look at the fixed costs of the business and identify where opportunities exist for reducing these.

Now, a word of warning.

I have noticed that cost cutting as an exercise often takes place under the direction of either an external advising accountant or a financial controller within the company itself.

Whilst the reduction of unnecessary cost is a front of mind role for such advisors, sometimes they are not fully aware of the knock-on impacts of their recommendations.

After all, no business ever grew purely by trimming costs!

It is important that the decision making on spend for a company is NOT, therefore, the exclusive remit of those working in the financial departments. It may be there ultimate decision, but it should not only have their knowledge applied.

This is because there are a number of important functions performed within a company that will always sit in the 'expenses' category on a profit and loss sheet but by rights should be placed under a totally separate category of 'Investments'.

That section doesn't exist on a profit and loss report, but in my view it should; and I don't mean assets (those rest firmly on the balance sheet).

The difference I am getting at here is that an 'Investment' in this context is something that you pay out for now but is fully intended to generate a return in the future, or will prevent a loss in the future. Examples include marketing (when done well), staff training, and research and development.

These are often critical functions for the future growth of a company, and if the bean counting cost cutters are given free rein on these, it can fundamentally stifle the future of a business.

If effective marketing is curtailed, this reduces enquiries, and that leads to lower sales, which leads to less gross profit, which leads to business slowing and other issues.

If staff training is stopped, performance declines, the competitive edge is lost, the business becomes commoditised, and the company loses position in the market.

If research and development is prevented, the company is overtaken, the value proposition declines, and the business slides from innovative leader to aging and losing laggard.

My point is that not everything with a cost is bad, but it can be very difficult to directly demonstrate the immediacy of the result that those elements bring. In longer term strategy, there has to be a degree of trust and a degree of forethought. It cannot simply be a case of culling costs line by line; the strategic consideration for the medium and longer term *must* also be considered. Else you end up with a business that profits today but dies tomorrow.

Having said that, it also isn't the case that you just act on speculation in all cases. A pragmatic, balanced view needs to be applied. Ask for the argument for maintaining that cost, and demand to understand the rationale. Only once you have an informed position should you make those decisions on what to cut and what to keep.

A real-world example here is to look at the impact of the recession on UK businesses during the 2009 financial crash. A number of rigorous studies have shown that companies that continued to market positively during that time actually survived in greater numbers, and in many cases grew at a faster rate subsequently, than those that reduced their spend or cut their marketing activity entirely.

I'd liken these important activities to breathing. You don't need more than you need, but opt for too little, and it quickly becomes painful and terminal!

Drawing the nine profit levers together to create the 'compound effect'

You may be thinking, 'That's quite a lot of things to work on – can't I just work on one or two?'

The answer is, 'Of course you can'. But before you take the 'easy path', I want to share with you something quite powerful that might inspire you to look at things a little differently.

So far, I have talked through the nine levers, and these are the basis for strategic decisions in your business that drive up profit. What I haven't yet done (except for the sales mix) is demonstrate to you how it works in the numbers.

You see, when you combine the driving metrics for your business into a sequence of stages, you start to see how profit really gets generated and how a compounding effect can occur.

When you focus exclusively on one number, you only get the impact of the improvement of that one number. However, when you focus on a set of connected numbers, you gain the benefits of compounding within your business profits.

Allow me to demonstrate!

Below is a profit generating sequence. This is the basis of a mathematical sequence that develops profit in your business...

DRIVERS = RESULT = PURPLE	START METRICS	STRATEGICALLY TARGETTED IMPROVEMENT	OUTCOME RESULT	COMPOUNDED INCREASE
NEW lead contacts	2000 X	+10%	2200 X	
Marketing Conversion	10% =	+10%	11% =	
NEW PROSPECT ENQUIRIES RESULTING	200 X	⇨	242 X	UP BY 21%
Sales Conversion Rate	50% =	+10%	55% =	
NEW CUSTOMERS RESULTING	100 X	⇨	133.1 X	UP BY 33.1%
Average value of a first year order	£2500 X	+10%	£2750 X	
Average number of orders in the first year	4 =	+10%	4.4 =	
TURNOVER FROM **NEW** CLIENTS	£1,000,000 X	⇨	£1,610,510 X	UP BY 61%
Gross Margin	25% =	+10%	27.5% =	
GROSS PROFIT FROM **NEW** CLIENTS	£250,000	⇨	£442,890	UP BY 77.1%

What this diagram is showing you is that an improvement of 10% to each of the six Driving KPIs for your business (those described in blue text in the left column) mathematically compounds to deliver an increase of 77.1% on gross profit.

This is just mathematics. Whatever the start figures are, the outcome would become the same with those changes applied... and that's important.

Whilst not every business can move all elements by 10% easily, equally not every business is limited to just 10% either. You can run the numbers with any percentage improvement you think realistic, and the formula will show the impact on gross profit.

Obviously, to take that forward to net profit simply requires a bit more consideration on other costs incurred to scale production or output to that level.

e.g.

What fixed costs would need to change to operate at that level (new buildings, vehicles, staff, etc).

This profit lever formula was based on new clients in this example, but the element from repeat and ongoing customers can also be calculated similarly.

You simply use the following sequence of metrics instead...

Active customers on the database

X

Nurture marketing effectiveness

=

Active customer enquiries

X

Sales conversion rate to existing customers

=

Repeat customers resulting

X

Average order value

X

Annual order frequency

=

Turnover

X

Gross margin

=

Gross Profit from existing customers

To look at the company holistically, you add together the relevant elements and produce overall metrics, i.e.

Turnover from new customers

+

Turnover from pre-existing customers

=

Turnover from all customers

This set of metrics is really useful as, depending on the stage of business you are at and the type of business you operate, you can strategically prioritise which numbers you can influence most effectively and how this would affect your company.

To get a bit more advanced, you can separate out the different revenue streams to show where your actions can have the greatest effect in terms of sales mix (as was shown earlier).

This model is well worth learning and applying.

Have fun with it!

Chapter 6 – Reflection and Exercise

	Our current metrics	Our target metrics
NEW lead contacts		
Marketing conversion		
NEW PROSPECT ENQUIRIES RESULTING		
Sales conversion rate		
NEW CUSTOMERS RESULTING		
Average value of a first year order		
Average number of orders in the first year		
TURNOVER FROM NEW CLIENTS		
Gross margin		
GROSS PROFIT FROM NEW CLIENTS		

N.B.

It may well be that you cannot *yet* complete all the numbers in this sheet. If that is the case, enter the ones you know, and set a realistic uplift target regardless.

Mathematics will not care that you don't yet have them all, and the impact is more likely if you start with some than none!

However, do also include some goals to set up the recording and reporting for the missing elements. The power is partly in being able to plan against known starting numbers.

Chapter 7

CONTROLLING THE FINANCES

As you are no doubt spotting, business is a game of numbers.

Inputs and outputs, if you like.

Finances are the most commonly tracked and reported upon numbers in business, but there is a huge problem for many small businesses.

The financial numbers they receive are *all* historical.

➤ Their profit and loss account tells them what happened last month, or last year.

➤ Their statement of cashflows tells them where money used to be and which direction it travelled.

➤ Their balance sheet shows them the balance of assets and liabilities as they were at a particular moment in time.

This is a problem. As far as I know, none of us has the ability to reverse time. Whilst there is a lot to be gained by understanding history, we cannot change it.

What business owners need to do is to work out not just how to see the past but also how to predict the future.

For some industries and businesses this is easier than for others, but for *all* it is something to strive towards. The common management accounting tools for predicting and planning for the future include:

1. Cashflow forecaster

2. Budget / P+L forecast

3. Sales forecaster

4. Creditor and debtor reports and action plans.

All are useful and have specific roles to play. Let's look at them in turn.

A **cashflow forecaster** is used to estimate the future available operating cash that a company will have (i.e. the liquid cash that they can access and use at any moment in time).

Operating cash is the lifeblood of business, and it's vital to understand the difference between technical profit on paper and real cash availability in the bank account.

Lots of businesses find that they are profitable in theory and bust in reality!

A classic example is Enron: a very large business that produced a technical profit but closed because it failed to manage cash and ran out of liquidity to function.

One aspect of cashflow forecasting that causes a slight challenge exists in many financial software programs, and it comes as a function of how they operate.

You see, the method is that once an invoice is raised within the system, it reviews the due date and assigns the income into the cashflow forecaster for that date. This makes sense, but doesn't take account of two factors.

First, clients all have their own payment habits, and most SME business owners are aware of them. For example, I know that some clients pay early each and every month, and others pay on the due date and never before.

This 'human behaviour' knowledge means that where I manage the cashflow forecaster entries manually, I actually increase the accuracy of the prediction.

I suspect that in time, the systems will become more intuitive and start to recognise the behaviours of various client accounts and take these behavioural differences into consideration when calculating likely available cash for the future.

Second, most accounting systems do not incorporate any expected income from clients for whom an invoice has not yet been raised. This makes any forecast that goes beyond the invoicing terms inaccurate (as it doesn't take into account any secured sales value that has not yet been invoiced). Again, I expect that if they have not already (and I may not be aware if they have!), these systems will become more adept at connecting 'won deals' from within a CRM system with the financial forecasting elements within financial software.

A simple cashflow forecaster outline is shown below to give you a feel for what they look like. It includes three main elements:

1. A sheet that details the various payments expected IN, e.g.

MONEY IN	Week 1	Week 2	Week 3	Week 4	TOTAL
Debtor 1	£1,000.00			£1,000.00	£2,000.00
Debtor 2		£4,000.00			£4,000.00
Debtor 3		£2,000.00	£2,000.00	£4,000.00	£8,000.00
Debtor 4	£3,000.00			£5,000.00	£8,000.00
Debtor 5		£2,000.00	£1,000.00	£3,000.00	£6,000.00
TOTAL	£4,000.00	£8,000.00	£3,000.00	£13,000.00	£28,000.00

2. A sheet that details the various payments expected OUT, e.g.

MONEY OUT	Week 1	Week 2	Week 3	Week 4	TOTAL
Creditor 1	£2,000.00			£1,000.00	**£3,000.00**
Creditor 2		£1,000.00	£1,000.00		**£2,000.00**
Creditor 3	£3,000.00	£2,000.00	£2,000.00		**£7,000.00**
Creditor 4		£6,000.00		£1,000.00	**£7,000.00**
Creditor 5		£5,000.00			**£5,000.00**
TOTAL	£5,000.00	£14,000.00	£3,000.00	£2,000.00	**£24,000.00**

3. A summary sheet that calculates the impact on the bank balance of incoming and outgoing cash, e.g.

	Week 1	Week 2	Week 3	Week 4	TOTAL
Start - bank account balance	£5,000.00	£4,000.00	-£2,000.00	-£2,000.00	
Money In	£4,000.00	£8,000.00	£3,000.00	£13,000.00	**£28,000.00**
Money Out	£5,000.00	£14,000.00	£3,000.00	£2,000.00	**£24,000.00**
Week End - resulting balance	£4,000.00	-£2,000.00	-£2,000.00	£9,000.00	Net flow this period
Overdraft / Credit / Other Available	£1,000.00	£1,000.00	£1,000.00	£1,000.00	
Maximum critical cash availability	£5,000.00	-£1,000.00	-£1,000.00	£10,000.00	**£4,000.00**

IMPORTANT DEMONSTRATION:

In the above example, you can see that the business is technically receiving more money than it is paying out during the four week period. *However*, when we look at the timing of the receipts and payments, there is a deficit in weeks 2 and 3 that is problematic. This is highlighted in pink and actually shows that the company would experience an overdrawn bank balance, beyond the agreed credit limit.

Not good!

In the next example, and having planned ahead for this cash deficit, the financial manager for this business made some calls, and some decisions; they agreed on payment extensions of one week with some of their suppliers and also contacted some clients pro-actively to motivate an early payment or two.

Here is the impact of 'seeing it coming' and 'taking preventative action'... all only made possible by the cashflow prediction bringing the issue to light in advance.

1. Adapted money *in* sheet: Debtor 4 and 5 paying sooner

MONEY IN	Week 1	Week 2	Week 3	Week 4	TOTAL
Debtor 1	£1,000.00			£1,000.00	£2,000.00
Debtor 2		£4,000.00			£4,000.00
Debtor 3		£2,000.00	£2,000.00	£4,000.00	£8,000.00
Debtor 4	£3,000.00	£2,500.00		£2,500.00	£8,000.00
Debtor 5		£2,000.00	£4,000.00		£6,000.00
TOTAL	£4,000.00	£10,500.00	£6,000.00	£7,500.00	£28,000.00

2. Adapted money *out* sheet: Creditor 4 and 5 being paid later

MONEY OUT	Week 1	Week 2	Week 3	Week 4	TOTAL
Creditor 1	£2,000.00			£1,000.00	£3,000.00
Creditor 2		£1,000.00	£1,000.00		£2,000.00
Creditor 3	£3,000.00	£2,000.00	£2,000.00		£7,000.00
Creditor 4		£4,000.00		£3,000.00	£7,000.00
Creditor 5		£2,500.00	£2,500.00		£5,000.00
TOTAL	£5,000.00	£9,500.00	£5,500.00	£4,000.00	£24,000.00

3. Adapted summary cashflow forecast sheet

	Week 1	Week 2	Week 3	Week 4	TOTAL
Start - bank account balance	£5,000.00	£4,000.00	£5,000.00	£5,500.00	
Money In	£4,000.00	£10,500.00	£6,000.00	£7,500.00	**£28,000.00**
Money Out	£5,000.00	£9,500.00	£5,500.00	£4,000.00	**£24,000.00**
Week End - resulting balance	£4,000.00	£5,000.00	£5,500.00	£9,000.00	**Net flow this period**
Overdraft / Credit / Other Available	£1,000.00	£1,000.00	£1,000.00	£1,000.00	
Maximum critical cash availability	£5,000.00	£6,000.00	£6,500.00	£10,000.00	**£4,000.00**

IMPORTANT TAKEAWAY POINT:

On these sheets, there are exactly the same amounts of money inbound and outbound as in the original. It is the timing that has been changed, and by doing so the company remains solvent and with available operating cash.

As you can see from the demonstration here, cashflow forecasting can prevent disaster and be very empowering for a business. In the example, the company is technically profitable during the period but could have suffered some very serious interruption were it not for a pro-active financial controller identifying and reacting positively to the threat.

Budgets / P+L Forecasters

The second document that is useful for predicting the future is the **budget.**

For many, the term budgeting is how they refer to cost management, but I believe that view is rather narrow. As we have discussed earlier in this book, no company ever grew by having its only strategy as cutting costs. In fact, as we saw, cutting the wrong 'investment costs' can be a real case of cutting off your business nose to spite your business face.

It's important to enable the driving facets of your business, as well as to spot and minimise over-spending.

I'd describe this as 'trimming the fat, but **not** the muscle' of your business.

So what does a profit and loss forecast look like? Pretty much the same as a historical profit and loss report!

The key difference, however, is that instead of one column of 'answers' showing what definitely did happen, in the forecaster version, there will be three columns.

1. The Intention (what you are planning to happen)

2. The Reality (what actually does happen)

3. The Variance (the difference between the two numbers)

N.B. *The Intention is the forecasting element, and the Reality and the Variance are only completed as time passes and those details become available.*

January

	Intention	Reality	Variance
Turnover	£90,000.00	£93,000.00	£3,000.00
Cost of Sales	£20,000.00	£30,000.00	+£10,000.00
Gross Profit	£70,000.00	£63,000.00	-£7,000.00
Fixed Costs	£40,000.00	£38,000.00	£2,000.00
EBITDA	£30,000.00	£25,000.00	-£5,000.00
Tax	£4,500.00	£4,000.00	-£500.00
Dividends	£20,500.00	£20,500.00	£0.00
Retained Profit	£5,000.00	£500.00	-£4,500.00

In this example you can see both a prediction (in the column marked intention) and an actual report (in the column marked reality) for a specific month.

There is a RAG system (red, amber, green) applied to the variance column to make it very easy for the business owners and managers to see quickly where the numbers are either better than expected, or worse. This is a very simple method, but it works well for most SMEs. Some similar planning, tracking, and reporting functionality exists in mainline financial software (accounting and bookkeeping) systems.

The budget document can of course be expanded and made more complex by separating out different revenue streams (e.g. widget 1 versus widget 2), cost centres (e.g. location 1 versus location 2) or functions (e.g. marketing, operations, and so on). In this case I have kept it simple for the purpose of demonstration, but do adapt your own to suit the situation. In my own real-world version, I have five revenue streams for five different marketing service categories that my business provides to customers.

A **sales forecaster** is designed to show what the pipeline of opportunities is like.

In some businesses, this is no more than a note or a spreadsheet showing which prospects will close within the next period and the expected sales figure, but for some these tools are really a work of science and art and make use of very refined CRM system funnels to manage a wide variety of data, stages, and likelihoods.

There are a number of reasons for achieving the latter version, including:

➤ Human memories are fallible, and perception is inconsistent.

➤ The CRM system prompts actions and can act as a partial manager as well as a financial predictor.

➤ The formal reports are more convincing for investors and shareholders.

➤ The software is easier for managing sales teams and multiple locations, categories, and so on.

➤ The software also insists data is more secure, compliant, accurate, and holistic.

BUT how do these systems actually work?

It's not as complex as many fear and is largely based on two elements: the quality of the data you enter and the accuracy (estimated or calculated) of the forecast.

As an example, below is a simple funnel for prospect stages and opportunity values.

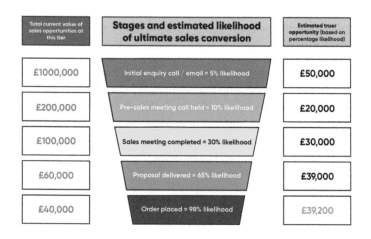

Total current value of sales opportunities at this tier	Stages and estimated likelihood of ultimate sales conversion	Estimated truer opportunity (based on percentage likelihood)
£1000,000	Initial enquiry call / email = 5% likelihood	£50,000
£200,000	Pre-sales meeting call held = 10% likelihood	£20,000
£100,000	Sales meeting completed = 30% likelihood	£30,000
£60,000	Proposal delivered = 65% likelihood	£39,000
£40,000	Order placed = 98% likelihood	£39,200

In this funnel diagram, an estimation of value at each stage has been applied.

For example, in the diagram below, the top level is showing £1,000,000 of opportunity based on the total prospect values tagged as being at that stage of the process.

This figure will be a summary of ALL the individual customers at that stage of progression, and all of the estimates on the best predicted order values from the sales personnel who have had those early stage interactions with those prospects. In simple terms, if there were to be 50 clients in that 'tier', then the average order estimate predicted by the sales person is set at £20,000 (50 x 20,000 = £1,000,000)

Except, of course that in most cases, this is a delusional view as not every enquiry results in an order. In fact, if we want to estimate the LIKELY revenue from that early stage, we need to consider the potential value, but multiply it by a LIKELIHOOD percentage based on it's distance from the metaphorical finishing line.

From this top tier of the funnel, it is perhaps 1 in 20 prospects who will ultimately end up buying from the company (5%).

In the diagram, you can see this adjustment being calculated: the £1,000,000 of total **potential** (left side) is multiplied by the 5% conversion estimate (middle section) and becomes £50,000 of **likely** value (on the right side).

This is how many CRM/sales pipeline systems work to give a more realistic view on the future performance of a business. I have always liked this approach as it is metrics-based and allows companies to be both targeted and also responsive when they start to see a stage causing a bottleneck in progression. It links really well with systemisation and staff training aspects of business.

It's also worth noting that this system is not entirely linear, as the value of prospective orders at each tier will vary throughout the year based on a number of factors including seasonality, time limited offers, promotions, and the level of sales follow up or effectiveness of the current team at progressing enquiries through.

Creditor and debtor reports and action plans are the final document for this section, and they are perhaps the most important of all for many businesses.

I say this because no matter what you plan for the future or what your sales pipelines suggest may happen moving forward, if you are currently experiencing a cashflow challenge, it's likely in some way that it's linked to debt or credit management.

Businesses don't tend to fail from a lack of forecasting, but they do tend to fail from a lack of cash. This isn't an option but a requirement.

WHAT ARE DEBTOR AND CREDITOR REPORTS?

Easy, they are simply summaries of who owes you money (or who you owe money to), when they (you) owe it by, and a calculation of how much is past due.

Normally these are reported as 'within terms', 30+, 60+ and 90+.

Within terms means that the invoices have been sent but your agreed terms to that customer have not yet been exceeded.

30+, 60+ and 90+ simply identify how much value and which customers have payments due to you that are now more than 30 days, 60 days, or 90 days.

These timings can be set differently but they are generally defaulted to this based on a normal credit term of 30 days, and many companies make payment runs every month (loosely 30 days also).

The key point is to be well informed by running these reports regularly and to be pro-active in keeping on top of your debtors.

For most, this is a simple case of designing an appropriate debt management system with consistent contact points (e.g. +1 day, + 7 days, + 14days and +30 days) which are coupled with consistent messaging (e.g. a call script, an email, another email, a formal legal letter). The right sequence of times, messages, and formats can vary a bit depending on the business you are running or those you deal with, but the central tenet should be this:

If you have met your side of the contract, then they should meet theirs.

That's it. No if's and no but's.

We are all in business to get paid, and a customer who doesn't pay is not a customer, but a debtor. Their bank balance is benefitting by the amount you are losing out on... and that's not right!

Things to watch for:

Over the years there have been a few occasions where I or my clients have hit headaches because of these common issues.

Here are a few pointers to watch for...

➤ Make sure that you credit check customers who will be receiving invoices that are larger than your 'comfort value' (this is the amount that it would be genuinely painful to experience a non-payment or substantially delayed payment for). Credit checking is easy to do, cost effective, and can help you pre-empt problem clients. If you identify one that may be a problem, you can still serve them if you wish; you may just want to arrange for payment in advance, low credit ceilings, or some other agreeable change to the normal financial practices for your business.

➤ Make sure you understand your client's payment runs and systems in advance of agreeing to serve them. Many are used to 'abusing' suppliers through tactics such as single date payment runs each month or having a cut-off date for 'authorised payments' for the next run.

➤ Make sure that you have *the* conversation. Often issues arise because a conversation around payment terms never happens, and the customer 'skims over' that aspect of the contract. Remember, it doesn't help if you are right but the bank account is still empty because of a misunderstanding.

➤ Learn who the accounts personnel are! It's surprising how often a little relationship sugar can sweeten your payment receipt timings. Be friendly, courteous, and helpful. Often these individuals have high workloads and receive little appreciation!

➤ Set the tone early. Debt recovery is the opposite to first aid. In first aid, you are advised to go to the quiet casualty first. In debt management, the business that is most communicative and pro-active in recovery tends to get paid first. If the early invoices to a new customer are not being paid to terms or look like they won't be, get pro-active. Provide reminders, give clear explanations of expectation, and where needed make those calls. Don't be afraid to bring a little ethics to bear – e.g. 'We have fulfilled our side of the agreement, and you promised that you would pay on time when we did so'. I have often found that drawing the aspect of personal integrity into question gets the job done – because now it's not a case of 'game playing' but of potentially reduced social and ethical standing for that individual.

CHAPTER 7 – REFLECTION AND EXERCISE

The following improvements need to be made in the management of our business financials:

Recording:

....

....

Reporting:

....

....

Interpretation and forecasting:

....

....

Debt management:

....

....

Cashflow management:

....

....

Target setting:

....

....

Chapter 8

MARKETING STRATEGY

Marketing is a *big* subject; so big, in fact, that Henry and I wrote a whole other book on the topic just a couple of years ago (*Growing by Design*, 2019).

For the purpose of this book, where we are aiming for a broader overview of business topics, we'll revisit some of the highlight concepts and add in a few fresh tips that we have discovered since completing that book.

MARKETING OBJECTIVES

Over the years, I have worked with a few hundred companies on their growth strategies. Almost all of those strategies have in one way or another required improved marketing results.

Yet, almost as universally, when we have first spoken about marketing with these companies (even those that had skilled academic marketers in their teams), there has been a problem.

The problem has been a lack of understanding what marketing is at its heart.

Marketing is a series of mechanisms designed to attract, progress, and maximise opportunities for business.

In the modern world of social media and digital marketing, where metrics are available by the bucket load, it helps a lot to remember that simple definition.

Why?

Well, because otherwise it's very easy to get distracted towards things that look good on a graph but don't actually make much difference in the real business environment for many SMEs.

I can't tell you how many social media gurus have talked at me in terms of likes, follows, and shares as if they are the ultimate outcomes. They aren't... they are part of the mechanism available, and one (of many) options to get the job done. For some businesses they will work brilliantly, and for others they will be largely pointless vanity metrics. It all comes back to understanding your audiences and how your clients like to interact, learn, and buy.

There is no 'one size fits all' solution to marketing – no one tactic or channel that is universally best. It takes effort to consider, to plan, and to select the right mix for your company... what I can do is show you a framework that will make those considerations simpler to pull together.

THE COMMON 10

When I first realised that most business owners were not marketers, and that many marketers were better technicians than strategists, I decided to start with some questions.

These questions included:

➤ What do you really want from your marketing?

➤ Why do you want that?

➤ What would achieving this allow you to do in your business and your life?

Often the answers were very straightforward. They included such things as:

'I want more sales, so that I can make more money, which would mean less stress at work and a better enjoyment of life away from the office.'

These answers were 'ok' but didn't really get to the heart of the matter. What I heard was 'I want better business results so that I can have better life results.' Whilst totally understandable, it wasn't very specific, and it left a whole load of unanswered 'How' questions.

After much mulling over of this challenge, I decided to reverse the question and asked myself, 'If I were to get a really helpful answer – one that conclusively told me what that business owner really needed – what would that look like?'

The answer I wrote became not just the basis for that book, but also the basis of working practices in two marketing agencies and a fundamental guidance pillar of my business coaching firm. It's called the Common 10, as that detailed answer included a breakdown of the 10 marketing objectives that are common to all businesses but are surprisingly rarely stated in this way!

The Common 10 are:

1. Improve your brand message and perception

2. Maximise your findability, visibility, and reach

3. Build your database

4. Nurture your prospects and enable enquiries

5. Increase your sales conversion

6. Maximise your sales values

7. Build your customer lifetime value

8. Capture and present your proof

9. Reactivate your past clients and prospects

10. Build and market through your alliance and introducer partnerships.

Opposite is a re-worked diagram to explain the relationship between the different components. This is closer to the intention of how a real-world marketing plan should come together than the earlier version of this model demonstrated.

I appreciate this is a somewhat complex image, so to help you wrap your head around the concept, here is a walkthrough text explaining how the elements sequence and some of the (generalised) thinking behind how it all works together...

The first thing to identify is that right now there are a number of potential customers in your marketplace: **a world of opportunity**.

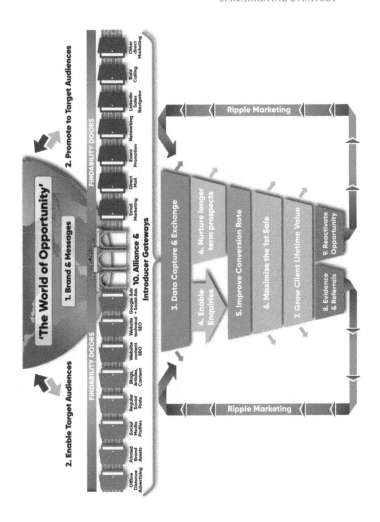

These opportunities may be new to the market and may not yet have explored their supplier options, they may be established and already have a supplier, or they may simply not be aware of the service or product you can offer and why they may even require it.

They are out there, and they haven't yet bought *from you*.

The first question you need to ask yourself about these many opportunities is

'Who do we want to talk to, and what do we want to say?'

This question is important, as whilst it is possible to talk to everyone with exactly the same tone and exactly the same message, the basis of great and influential marketing is that it is tailored to each audience. For example, you probably speak differently to your grandparents than to your spouse, and differently still to your boss, or your doctor. The style, tone, deference, language, and perhaps even speed or volume changes.

The questions of 'who?' and 'how?' are the basis of any decent conversation, whether for a business or for an individual. If the message, tone, language, and so on is considered relevant, interesting, and perhaps event exciting, the chances of a progressing relationship with a prospect are increased.

As a further example, the context for the conversation is critical. If you are a caterer and you know you are speaking with a vegetarian prospect, you will almost automatically default to speaking about what you know is relevant. Whilst your meat dishes may be fantastic, you know they are less relevant and switch the content to suit the precise audience. This same premise applies to all marketing, and yet only a small proportion of businesses actually provide content which is specialised to each known audience. More often they approach it from the perspective of what they provide, rather than who they serve, and the issue with that is that the language used is that of the supplier and not of the recipient. It may seem a small point, but I promise you that once you master speaking the language of your prospect, you'll see engagement and conversion rates rise!

So, who do you want to talk to, and how would they like to hear you?

Remember that some of the conversations will be decidedly one-sided to start with. Your contacts will be metaphorically 'speaking with' your website, your blog, your flyers, or even your business card. What do you want those central messages to say, and how do you want that initial impression to be made?

This exercise is really all about branding and target audience segmentation.

Once you have established your brand identity and values and shaped them to match the specific audiences you want to influence, you'll be well underway.

This is Objective 1: 'Improve your brand and messages', and it is the foundation upon which the rest of your marketing rests. Don't shortcut it, as it will cost you dearly to do so!

Key aspects to cover include:

➤ Brand identity (what character, language, and imagery?)

➤ Vision and mission (what is the intended legacy and experience?)

➤ Brand values (what does your business stand for?)

➤ Target audiences (who are they; what are their avatars?)

➤ Where will your brand be present and recognised?

Objective 2 is to increase your visibility, findability, and reach.

Your potential customers will come in one of two main ways.

They will find you, or you will find them.

For the former, this is where your company visibility and findability are crucial.

Findability is simply the ease with which a prospect can come into contact with your business information, influential materials, or personnel. This can be online or offline. There are a multitude of ways of increasing that likelihood, and some of these are indicated in the diagram as doorways on the left hand side (offline advertising, social media, blog, website, etc.)

Visibility is the level of presence and authority that exists within those different channels and platforms. Is it just a website, or a website that ranks #1 for two hundred keywords? Is it an advert in the back of a parish magazine, or on the front page of The Times? Visibility is about making your presence obvious and gaining a higher level of traction and traffic as a result.

In the modern digital world, this is also substantially about achieving more effective and broader referencing within the search engine results pages (SERPS) using strategic options such as SEM (search engine marketing, e.g. Google Ads) social media PPC (pay per click, e.g. Facebook Ads), and SEO (search engine optimisation) for websites and other searchable content such as videos on YouTube. This is a massive subject and can be highly technical.

Reach is the number of contacts and connections you are achieving and how the message is shared onwards and outwards. Is the content influential? Does it have a viral aspect to send the contact levels skyrocketing? Is there some influencer who can propagate the messages forwards?

Reach also includes your own direct marketing. This is where we don't rely on the phone ringing inbound but take steps to deliver our messages in a targeted way to those we believe have a prospective interest. Direct marketing nowadays takes a very wide range of approaches.

Whichever channel or methodology you choose, it is worth developing a content calendar to outline the key messages you want to communicate throughout the year, and a campaigns calendar which will be more related to events or specific promotions. Content leads to engagement and traffic. Campaigns lead to uptake on offers and orders.

Objective 3 is to build your database.

It's a strange thing, but lots and lots of business owners and their staff literally throw away customers.

Every year, they gain the contact details of prospective customers from events, networking, and other areas, and then throw them away. Business card after business card ends up in the trash. Emails and telephone contact pads by the bucket load disappear forever. It's madness!

If you go to the effort of speaking with a prospect, or even a lead, then do everything within your power to gather the contact information and record it.

Obviously, being conscious of GDPR*, you then need to manage that information and ensure you protect it suitably and communicate only in legitimate ways.

The General Data Protection Regulation (GDPR) is a legal framework that sets guidelines for the collection and processing of personal information from individuals who live in the European Union (EU) or UK.

It's one of my greatest business regrets that I wasn't more self-disciplined about the capture and use of data in my early business days. There are literally thousands of contacts that I have wasted... and having spoken with dozens of other business owners, I know I'm not alone!

Nowadays I am much more systematic.

I have a CRM system for recording details and various tools for maintaining communication and ensuring ongoing permission for communication is achieved.

DATA CAPTURE VERSUS DATA EXCHANGE

Lots of business owners I speak to will tell me they have a well-managed database, but on inspection, it turns out they have a well-managed client database. This might seem like semantics, but it isn't.

Client databases are easy. In most cases these are actually invoice lists for customers. They are stored as part of the accounts system, and unless that is connected to the marketing system, it has little value in terms of generating future enquiries and orders.

By contrast, a FULL database has the details of all contacts with the company and will often be able to be filtered by a range of factors that are beneficial when it comes to marketing (both for new clients and also for lifetime value). These databases include details such as the source of the opportunity (which campaign or channel they provided details through) as well as all the contact details, and perhaps a range of other useful details (such as a LinkedIn or other social handle).

In the modern world, these databases are now often best managed through CRM systems (customer relationship management software), and the advanced versions of these can even make use of choice-based architecture and artificial intelligence too!

For SME business owners, it is really a case of doing the basics, and doing them well.

➤ Make sure that your marketing materials (findability based or direct based) have a motive for the leads to share their details and permissions with you.

➤ Make use of a system such as Hubspot, Zoho, Salesforce, or another CRM tool to record the contact information and to help categorise the opportunities.

➤ Make sure you create a communication pattern with your prospects that is suitable to their situation and your marketing intentions – both at the outset and for the longer term.

Objective 4 is to nurture prospects and enable their enquiries.

Not every prospect will make an enquiry immediately.

It doesn't mean they have no value just because they aren't yet ready to buy *yet*, but many businesses only ever focus upon the immediate opportunities. This may be a 'hungry person's need to feed now' mindset, but it isn't a great strategy for long term success.

Staying in touch with a prospect who fits the profile but who hasn't yet taken the leap to share their needs and make that enquiry with you is a sure-fire way to stack the pipeline for the future.

Whether it's a matter of making a note to call back, sending a periodic email to stay in touch, or making it a full blown progression campaign to nudge them over time, it's important not to let them drop off your radar. This slower-moving prospect pipeline will eventually drop through the stages, and if you work hard at expediting their progress, you'll enjoy the results of not just the immediate chances but also the nurtured pipeline.

I like to think of it as drinking water and treacle. The water comes straight through the funnel, but if I also warm the treacle, that will make it through too… and that makes the drink sweeter overall.

As a personal story, one of my best clients came as a result of a five-year nurturing process.

I first met them when they attended an event I was presenting.

I followed up with a phone call shortly after, and they said, 'We're not ready.'

I put them on the email list for future events and contacts.

Over the next couple of years, I saw them at a number of other speaking events I was presenting at and always made sure to say hello and check on their progress.

I sent a Christmas card or two and emailed some interesting articles for their industry when I saw them as relevant.

I then saw them at a networking event and made sure to say Hi.

Eventually, almost out of the blue, I got a message that simply said, 'We're ready now; give me a call!'

Now not every opportunity will take five years, but also not everyone transacts on day one either. Some take persistence and a willingness to work the relationship even when unsure of the precise timeframe for opportunity. In this case I knew the company was a great prospect, but the initial timing was poor. It would have been easy to ignore and move on to the next obvious immediate opportunity, but I would have made a mistake and missed out.

Getting the balance right between active enquiry management and prospect nurturing is important. Once the momentum is built up on the slow-burners, you'll see that trickle of opportunity start to become a regular source of enquiries for the future, and that, in turn, makes life a lot less pressured to win the 'immediate needs' every time.

Some of the easiest ways to win longer term prospects is to create a regular communication method that includes a suitable mix of promotions, education, trust building, value add messages, and personal correspondence. Most often this is done through emails, newsletters, networking or personal contacts, or regular event invitations. Whatever your business, having a system to stay in touch with slower-moving prospects is essential if you want to benefit longer term.

The second element to this section is enquiry enablement.

Enquiry enablement includes a range of methods by which you gather information about the prospect and provide them with the opportunity to match their needs with your solutions.

Whichever form of ongoing communication you have chosen to ensure that your message and opportunity stays front of mind with your prospect, it's equally important that you remember to ask the question, 'Do you want to discuss the potential for solving that need with us?'

It's not always that blunt, and can be phrased a number of ways, but that is always the outcome you are seeking. A next step towards engagement.

Examples of that 're-phrased question' include:

➤ Would you like a free review?

➤ Have a no-obligation chat with our team

➤ Take up our offer of a free demonstration

➤ Reply to this email to get more information

➤ Use the chat box to ask any questions

...and so on. The key point being that nurturing is great, but you do need to include some form of call to action frequently if you are to prompt a reaction. Simply providing the information and hoping for the phone to ring or the email to ping is a *very* slow, and, in my experience, less effective approach for SMEs.

Better to ask the question and motivate a response. Open up the doorway, but also ring the bell for them.

Objective 5 is to increase your sales conversion.

Really great salespeople all possess one common trait. They are fantastic at *preventing* objections.

Note I said preventing, not handling. There is a *big* difference.

You see, the truly great sales person understands their prospect well enough to pre-empt the vast majority of potential objection issues and the timing at which they generally arise, managing them *in advance*.

How?

Well, part of it is being a great listener and someone who is highly observant. This allows them to learn all the time from their prospects' behaviour and responses.

But it also goes much deeper and often involves the 'communal brain' of the entire company. It isn't just sales people that are responsible for future sales.

This is because the best way to make a future sale is to create a happy customer today and to understand all the reasons why that may be prevented.

This might be a function of making amazing products that do what they say they will and more, or also through delivering a fantastic service. Equally, it might be as simple as making sure that the invoice is sent on time and is accurate, or making sure that the customer service desk answers the phone quickly and politely. It could even be that the waiting room is tidy and has a drinks machine.

Every step in the customer journey needs to be seamless, and when it isn't or where there is potential for it not to be, you need to recognise that as a 'fear factor' for a client.

My point is that businesses provide an experience, and if that *entire* experience is positive and professional, then the resulting client experience will make future sales much easier. Giving the sales person real stories that can be told that address the concerns of prospects is a massively powerful toolkit. Understanding where that fairy-tale story could (and perhaps elsewhere has) become a customer nightmare helps you understand their fears better.

Personally, I like to map out the idealised customer sales journey and then to highlight where objections tend to arise and what intervention or asset can precede that to reduce the likelihood of it happening again or of being a genuine 'derailer' rather than just a 'hesitator'.

A 'derailer' is something that results in a firm 'no'.

A 'hesitator' is something that gives them pause for thought or can delay matters until it has been resolved or reassured.

An example follows, and I have based this one on a car retailer.

The swim-lanes included are for each role that has interaction during the initial enquiry management stage of the business system. Within each 'lane' are the process steps that are to be completed by each relevant person. You'll note that there are expected actions for the customer/prospect also.

In this system, you can see that the majority of first step actions are for the receptionist. These include the 'Meet and Greet' process and various others. This document is designed to show the overview of the system and is not getting into the 'how to' (or procedure) level of detail. It is aimed at showing how the different steps sequence, who is involved, and who the next actions are to be completed by.

On the bottom right of some process stages, you can see some other icons. Those icons are explained in more detail below the main swim-lane image; in this example, they relate largely to scripts or documents, but in other system maps, they can also include software and other relevant tools that are required to complete the associated tasks.

This system map starts and finishes with an oval icon. This is called a terminator, and simply indicates that start or finish point. In this example, you can see that there are further actions to complete, as the final point states – 'move on to relevant sales system'. At this stage, the sales person would need to view the next system map to see full details of what the next stages would be.

The reason for the break is to keep the scale of processes easy to use and so you can see quickly where you are at in the system. It is also often pragmatic to separate when the systems move on to involving different staff members – e.g. the vehicle preparation team for the test drive and the financial team for arranging a lease deal. (See the diagram overleaf.)

By mapping out the system, you start to identify where actions have a purpose.

For example, providing a customer with a hot drink and a comfortable environment allows for a small delay in supplying a sales person to help them. It also allows for the sales person to prepare for a moment or two with the initial needs already established. The provision of information packs starts to answer the common questions, and the imagery starts to excite the customer about the experience to come.

In this approach it also allows you to review how current objections may be occurring and what could be done to address them. As an example, let's imagine that the feedback was that customers were still being frustrated by the delay in providing a skilled and knowledgeable sales person to interact with.

Perhaps with a very small adjustment, the receptionist could notify the sales team manager *before* taking the customer to the waiting area for a drink. This may involve a small step of adding in a process for making an inter-department telephone call and reflecting the needs the customer has to that manager verbally. This would expedite that requirement and save a minute or two. It is these refinements that reduce related objections.

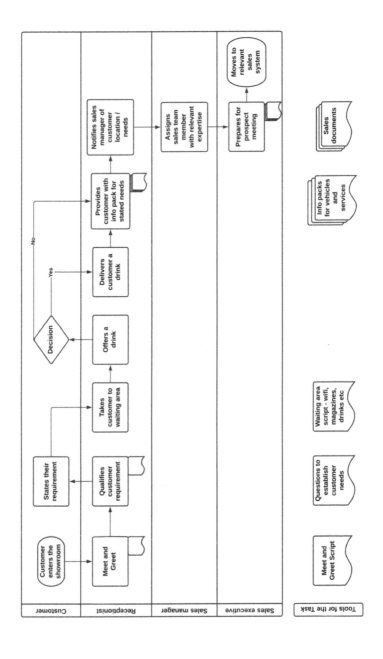

If the objection were to be 'I can't afford it', then perhaps the introduction of the finance support team at an earlier stage would help, or inclusion of finance examples in the information pack. As you can see, the key is to identify not just what the objections are, but when they arrive. By doing so you can either adapt a behaviour or provide a relevant asset to help address it early, and that matters.

Handling the objection *before* it is raised is the most effective way of avoiding any emotional negativity during the sales process.

There is a lot more on the topic of sales conversion, and indeed in sales skills for the salesperson, but for now I hope this has given you a taster on how objections can be reduced and on the systematic nature for doing so.

Objective 6 is to maximise the sales value.

It seems obvious, doesn't it, when I say that we should meet all the needs of our customers that we can.

Reality, however, is very different.

There are many occasions where sales teams simply serve the first stated requirement of the customer and do not dig deep enough to uncover all the others just below the surface. Worse than that, the account handlers then compound that mistake by only ever following up a customer about that requirement.

For example, for five years a garage follows up a customer who initially asked for an MOT, and all they ever talk to that customer about is an MOT. What about the servicing, bodywork, tyres, fuel cleaning, and other services??

This is a missed goldmine of opportunity!

The best method of avoiding this pitfall is to identify the most usual cross- and up-sells and make them an integral part of the enquiry management and sales systems.

When done badly, this can result in a barrage of questions, seemingly unrelated to the original query a customer makes. When done well, it's like a well-choreographed dance, where each step feels natural and intentional.

Review all the contact points you have with potential customers (new or previous) and identify where relevant questions or research can be conducted to give you the 'full picture'.

Then consider what the best timing and method of introducing cross- and up-sell potential into the dialogue will be. Using customer case studies is a fantastic way of doing this as it not only educates on what other services or products customers have bought, but it also allows you to subtly embed the reasoning behind those buying decisions.

The secondary element is to continue the education of your prospects and customers well beyond the direct interaction you may have with them early on. Using those regular newsletters, emails, calls, and other contact methods to stay in touch; learn about additional or emerging customer needs; and provide information on how they can buy more, and more often is important for achieving maximised sales.

Objective 7: Increase your Customer Lifetime Value (CLV).

Managing clients for the long term does take some effort on your side of the equation.

Remember that customers love to buy but hate to be sold to, so be careful to make sure you are seen as a valuable guide and adviser and not as a classic 'salesperson'.

Present opportunities, new learnings, insights, and recommendations. Use examples to engage emotion and generate aspiration and visualisation within your prospects.

Two great tools for making this happen are a customer focused content calendar and a campaign calendar (as were also mentioned in the visibility, findability, and reach objective – there with a view to communicating with new potential customers).

Generating the maximum return from your customers each and every year does require some planning ahead, and whilst you can set the campaigns calendar with relative confidence a year in advance, the content calendar needs to be a little more short term. Just imagine the shifts that have taken place this year in response to COVID-19 and Brexit!

IMPORTANT: For many start up and early year businesses, the focus of their marketing is almost exclusively on the top part of the Common 10 diagram. They invest a lot of time and money in 'buying a new customer'.

However, if they don't look after and manage that customer for the long term it is a seriously false economy.

Assuming your business products and services allow for repeat purchases or at least secondary purchases from your customers, you have already likely spent on the hard part of marketing and it would be criminal to not capitalise on your investment. By this I mean that the retention of existing customers for secondary and further sales is often cheaper than buying a new customer for the first time, every time.

Objective 8: Capture and present your proof.

We've seen within the conversion rate section that having the experiences of previous customers can be really helpful for steering the future behaviours of prospects who have not yet bought.

Part of this comes down to the natural human 'community' persuasion principle.

In his fantastic short video 'The six principles of persuasion', Robert Cialdini explains how as a species, human beings prefer not to be isolated in their decision making. It is more common for a person to follow a decision they have already seen made than to pioneer a fresh direction without any evidence of success being available beforehand. It's a fact that we prefer to follow than to lead.

Just think about your own buying behaviour. I'm willing to bet that before you book a hotel, or a restaurant, or in fact most things, you do a little research and you see what others experienced before you. Whether it is TripAdvisor, Which?, Trust-a-Trader, website reviews, or Karen on Facebook that you seek an opinion from, it's likely that having that evidence to hand is influential on your next step.

Will it be advance, retreat, or change direction?

It's the same for your prospects.

They are interested in what people have to say about you, almost more than what you can say about yourself. This is because (and take it in the spirit I mean it), they trust those people more than they trust you right now. The sales person is always less trusted than someone who appears to have nothing to gain from sharing their opinion about you.

As a sales person, you are intrinsically distrusted at the outset because they know you stand to gain if they go ahead with an order. Not nice, but that's the rub I'm afraid, my friends!

The best you can do is to gather together all those valued opinions that your prospects care about, in the greatest volume and the strongest terms possible, and make them highly visible to those prospects.

When you control and collate the narrative, there is less chance of them finding that rogue negative review, and you are also helping your prospect by taking a task off their 'to do' list – you've done the research and delivered it so that they don't have to.

What I mean by all this is that you need to solicit feedback and capture those stories and case studies that prove your argument for you. Gather it together and place it positively and intentionally at all stages of the sales process, not just at the ultimate decision point.

By the time your prospect has seen great testimony, lots of online reviews, fantastic case studies, and customer experience statistics that make their decision a no-brainer, well, that's when your gathered proof starts gathering you more orders and less price resistance.

In terms of presentation of proof, there are several locations and options. Here are a few worth mentioning:

➤ Your own website. This can be uploads of client testimonials, case studies, videos, or an iframe bringing in the details from other active review sites.

➤ Review sites. Examples are Which?, Trust Pilot, and Check-a-Trade. Which ones exist for your industry?

➤ Social media. There are review ratings available on Facebook and other social platforms. These can be very powerful as when you are reviewed, the reviewer's audience also sees what they had to say.

➤ Directories. Some directories don't just have a listing but also customer review sections.

➤ Association sites and networking sites. Lots of associations and networking groups have online listings and the option for customers to place reviews about your business.

The core point to consider here is what a customer needs to see in terms of reassurance. It isn't just a case of getting a rating level, but also attempting to gather and present customer stories and testimonials that actively work to reduce the prospect's fears of dealing with your industry or your business specifically.

If you had a historic poor reputation for timekeeping, get 50 reviews that prove you are respectful of time and how you are now the most reliable business in town... address the worries, by getting customers and advocates to present your case for you.

They are seen as independent, more credible, and more influential than you can ever be for yourself.

Objective 9 is to reactivate past customers and prospects.

Hopefully by now you have recognised the value of not taking a 'one and done' mindset – i.e. 'One contact or one sale, and the relationship is done.'

Building a business is about developing lifelong positive relationships. More seeking a set of happy marriages than transient one night stands.

Past customers are those who have fallen silent or have stopped buying. Depending on your business, this might be obvious within a few months (e.g. a supermarket preference switch) or a few years (a customer using a different painting and redecorating service for their next home overhaul).

Whatever the timeframe over which you recognise that a customer goes from being 'active' to 'inactive', it's good to take action. It's amazing how often a personalised prompt or a reward-based motive can get that customer back into the green and shopping with you again.

A recent example for our own company was an e-shot we sent out for a customer. This was sent to the inactive database and yielded three enquiries worth around £10,000 each – from customers that our client said were inactive.

They weren't inactive... what they were was neglected!

It's a sad state of affairs that most customers who become inactive or move to other suppliers do so because of a term called 'perceived indifference'. They simply started to feel that you no longer cared about them and that someone else appeared more interested.

Reactivation marketing is a great way of contacting this group of disassociated customers and saying, 'We miss you; please come back.'

It's a straightforward tactic, and you can use a range of channels and tactics to apply it, but just make sure you do it! It's fertile ground, and it's quick wins!

Objective 10 is to build and market through alliance partners and introducers.

Strategic alliances are businesses that are non-competitive to your own. This means that they serve the same target audience as you do, but they meet different needs.

As an example, a domestic gardener serves homeowners and tenants of properties in the local area. A domestic plumber will also serve that same audience, but they are non-competing.

The clients of the gardener may well have a need for plumbing at some stage, and vice versa. There exists, therefore, an opportunity for reciprocal or co-operative marketing and referencing.

A simple example of a tactic that each could employ would be to include a 'trusted partner' scheme whereby they introduce their clients to the other supplier on a reciprocal basis. This might be achieved by using a Thank You card on completion of work for their client and including a message such as the one below:

'Dear Mr Jones,

We have really enjoyed working on your garden this week and were thrilled to hear how happy you are with the new layout and fresh plants.

Over the years our business has grown on reputation, and we know it isn't always easy to find great tradespeople to help when you need it.

With that in mind, I wanted to introduce you to XYZ Plumbers, a local company run by my friend David Smith. David has done a lot of work for clients of ours, and we know his team are fantastic and reliable.

> *As a client of ABC Gardening, we have arranged a 'new customer voucher' for you to use when you next have a need for a plumbing service. Simply give David's team a ring on 01234 567890 and they will be happy to honour the value on the enclosed voucher.*
>
> *I hope this small gift helps you, and we look forward to working with you again in the near future.*
>
> *Yours faithfully,*
>
> *Mark Jones*
>
> *ABC Gardening'*

As you can see, this is a very easy-to-apply tactic that has no cost unless a new client arrives... and in this way, with almost no acquisition cost for either party. It carries an implicit personal recommendation and testimony and a value add for the customer that re-affirms the experience they have already had with the first supplier.

This is the most basic form of alliance introduction, but as SMEs become a bit more advanced, there are opportunities such as backlinking on websites to help each other's SEO, guest blogging to raise credibility, email marketing with reciprocal offers and recommendations, social media endorsement or sharing, joint events or webinars, and a whole host of other ways to help raise the profile and order volumes of partners in a non-competing way.

This partnership marketing approach does not, however, tend to happen by accident. It requires a specific type of approach to develop that opportunity and to advance the relationship from stranger to referrer.

Some things to consider *before* partnering your marketing:

➤ Is the alliance partner non-competing?

➤ Do they have a solid and positive reputation?

➤ Have you interviewed several existing customers to fully understand their experience and to gain confidence in this being a good referral to give?

➤ Are these alliance partners pro-active marketers with a large or at least highly relevant contact database?

➤ Have you experienced their service for your yourself/trialled it so that you can confidently refer?

➤ Do you share values and ethical standards?

➤ Do you believe that they will do what they say they will? (This is essential as alliance partnerships are not one-sided. The vital aim is that you promote them to your contacts and they do the same.)

➤ Have you discussed relevant activities and talked through aligned campaigns, content, and other efforts to introduce one another in a systemised way (it should not be sporadic or opportunistic but part of the regular marketing activities for you both)?

➤ Have you trained your alliance partner on what a good referral is and how to position you, and provided them with relevant core tools (such as the voucher and card above) to help them succeed? Make it easy for them.

Again, there is more to add, but these basic pointers should help.

Those points do not, however, cover one of the critical challenges in this section... how do I get to speak with these potential alliances in the first place?

You are right to ask that one! It's easy to get wrong, and many business owners I have spoken with have asked potential partners, 'Would you like to promote me to your customers?'

Strangely enough, the answer is almost universally 'No' as almost no business owner has lots of spare time to promote another business as a favour.

It comes back to the old question of 'What's in it for me?'

Better perhaps to ask, 'Would you be interested in me referring my client base to you? It seems we are non-competing, and if we can find a suitable benefit to us both in doing that, I'd be happy to do so.'

This is more likely to lead to your alliance partner's interest and is only intended as the start of the process. All of the above bullet pointed items ultimately need to come to bear, but the start is a conversation based on beneficial gain for both parties. It's a balanced alliance mindset, similar to the contractual balance we mentioned earlier – 'I'll do this for you, if you'll do this for me.'

For that reason, it's always worth writing down all agreed actions properly and professionally and, where relevant, even creating a partnership agreement document to record what each side is committing to do and how things such as data will be managed to ensure GDPR compliance and so on.

I don't want the system to become a barrier to action for you here, but there are some realities that require that professional consideration, and GDPR/data security is one of the main elements that both parties need to be confident about and happy with before starting any reciprocal marketing. This is not an excuse for sharing data, and that element needs due diligence to ensure you, your partner, and your customers are all respected and secure.

THE VALUE OF MARKETING TOOLKITS

One of the biggest mistakes that I see in SME marketing efforts is the constant 'start from scratch' approach.

What I mean by this is that a business owner has a marketing idea, they create a tool that is designed specifically for that individual campaign, it is used once, and then is discarded or filed away somewhere never to be seen again.

One key aspect of business growth, as we'll see later on, is the ability to create systems that reduce and minimise the requirement for rework.

As a simple example, recently for one of the marketing agencies I am a director in, we were looking at creating some specialised website templates for one industry sector. Before we started on that project, I asked, 'How many websites have we built for that sector in the past, and how many have we seen that have been created by competitors?' The answer was 'Quite a few actually.'

By then exploring which elements were consistently required and what the common aspects of those sites were (e.g. they all include customer case studies, and they all make use of a chat function), we were able to identify where some previously-invested-in components could be mirrored and included into the new template. This saved a fair number of hours and in no way reduced the quality of the finished products.

This same thinking applies to any marketing asset that has the potential for re-use or easy adaption.

Then there is the option for re-purposing. This is a vital element of efficiency in marketing! By re-purposing, I mean re-working content or campaigns into a fresh format.

As an example, a customer testimonial video can be adapted into a pdf written testimonial with static images, as well as content for a website page or a blog, as well as short quotes being drawn from the audio to use as either soundbites or as the basis for social media posts.

The initial investment in gathering the story, content, or other asset can be used across a variety of formats and channels more cost effectively and in a more leveraged manner than just the 'one and done' approach.

It is astounding to me how often I am speaking with businesses that have been running for several years and yet when I ask what their marketing toolkit has in it, the answer is very often a website, a social media page, a business card, and, if we are lucky, some form of brochure or pop-up banner. After several years of marketing effort, it would make sense to expect there to be a library of assets and resources available that can we re-worked, re-used, updated, or adapted to expedite the next campaign or to act as a basis for consistent content presentation... but that isn't what happens in most cases.

The idea of creating proper 'marketing toolkits' is connected with the Common 10 strategic model. In its simplest form, the idea is that for each area of the model, you should aim to develop a core set of templates or re-useable assets. By doing so, the never-ending and highly cost inefficient 'every time is the first time' can be curbed. Your marketing can become 80% based on consistent approaches and re-worked/freshened up tools, and 20% can be for brand-new, breaking-the-mould materials.

On the next page is how the toolkits might line up with the model:

Website & SEO
Toolkit ___/10
Strategy ___/10

Visibility & Findability
Toolkit ___/10
Strategy ___/10

Branding + Core Messages
Toolkit ___/10
Strategy ___/10

Alliances & Introducers
Toolkit ___/10
Strategy ___/10

Direct Marketing
Toolkit ___/10
Strategy ___/10

Enquiry Management
Toolkit ___/10
Strategy ___/10

Data Capture & Exchange
Toolkit ___/10
Strategy ___/10

Prospect Nurturing
Toolkit ___/10
Strategy ___/10

Sales Conversion & Value Maximisation
Toolkit ___/10
Strategy ___/10

Customer Lifetime Value
Toolkit ___/10
Strategy ___/10

Referrals + Referencing
Toolkit ___/10
Strategy ___/10

Past Customer & Prospect Reactivation
Toolkit ___/10
Strategy ___/10

In the above diagram, you'll see that I have also included a self-rating scorecard so that you can quickly and easily rate your current marketing. I've kept it really basic for speed. Simply provide a subjective rating out of 10 for two elements:

First, do you have clear, effective, systemised strategies for attacking those marketing objectives (0 is none whatsoever, 5 is some and they are not great, 10 is all are nailed and brilliant… and any shades of grey you want to apply between!)?

Second, do you have a set of tools and resources that effectively support those strategies and can be easily updated, re-used, or refined for future iterations?

SUMMARY ON THE COMMON 10

As I mentioned at the start of this chapter (and yes, I know it's been a long chapter!), the Common 10 is the basis for one of my other books, *Growing by Design*. I have touched on the various objectives here but have not gone into as much depth or even all the same elements as are covered in that book.

If marketing and sales strategy are a significant part of your future business growth plans (and that's very likely), I would encourage you to read that book also. It addresses the topics in more detail and from a different viewpoint, so will help you deepen your understanding of these concepts.

Chapter 8 – Reflection and Exercise

Our strategy needs to be developed for the following areas of the Common 10...

Branding and Core Messages: YES / NO

If YES, your number 1 idea is: ....

Findability, Visibility, and Reach: YES / NO

If YES, your number 1 idea is: ....

Database Building: YES / NO

If YES, your number 1 idea is: ....

Prospect Nurturing: YES / NO

If YES, your number 1 idea is: ....

Sales Conversion: YES / NO

If YES, your number 1 idea is: ....

Maximising Sales Values: YES / NO

If YES, your number 1 idea is: ....

Increasing Customer Lifetime Value: YES / NO

If YES, your number 1 idea is: ....

Capturing and Presenting Proof: YES / NO

If YES, your number 1 idea is: ....

Past Client Reactivation: YES / NO

If YES, your number 1 idea is: ....

Developing Alliances: YES / NO

If YES, your number 1 idea is: ....

Chapter 9

SALES STRATEGY

Whilst sales is included within the Common 10 model of the prior chapter, and I have already addressed some elements of sales mapping, there is more that is worth covering here.

Specifically, I want to talk about the mindsets of prospects, sales people, and customers.

Let's start with prospect motivations.

For a prospect, the motivations (as shared within Chapter 5 – improving value acceptance) are primarily based around 'pain relief' or 'gains'. Understanding which of these you are dealing with will have a significant impact on how you choose to position your service or product. After all, it's important to acknowledge that the 'fear of loss is greater than the desire to gain'.

In fact, loss aversion is an important concept that is linked with prospect theory. Kahneman and Tversky (1979) expressed this in the phrase 'losses loom larger than gains'. It is estimated that the pain of losing is twice as powerful, in a psychological sense, than the pleasure of gaining.

Twice as large!

As an understanding of motive and influence, that recognition is huge!

Henry, my co-author for this book, often refers to **'grazing the knees'** of prospects in a sales environment.

He means that through effective questioning, the use of emotive language, and encouragement of customer visualisation (mentioned earlier), the prospect reached a position of feeling uncomfortable with their current situation and now holds a positive desire to move towards a new comfort zone (with the sales solution as the pathway).

This isn't as unkind a process as it might at first seem.

Nothing has actually changed for the prospect other than their acknowledgement of a situation and a clarity on the need and desire for change. No pain has been actually applied.

There has just been an exploration of what no change looks and feels like.

This funny meme encapsulates why it is so important!

Sales is simply a sequence of questions applied well:

Good questions, sequenced well, matched with provision of information about a solution and envisioning of a better future once that is in place.

SALES POSITIONING WITH A PROSPECT

The start point for any effective sales meeting is a positioning statement. This is where you (as the chairperson) get to set the tone of the meeting and to direct the order. It's not as difficult as you may think to do that either.

The first order of duty is to gain permission to chair.

Often, the perceived balance of power sits automatically with the customer, i.e. they have control as ultimately it is their decision that matters.

However, it's also true to say that in many cases, the customer does not have the experience of how these types of meetings run best. After all, as a professional sales person, it is likely that unless the buyer is a full time procurement specialist, you will have been involved in more meetings of this type than they have.

Certainly this is the case for most B2C (Business to Consumer) engagements.

Even if your prospect is a full time procurement manager, they still don't have the insight on how to best experience your sales process, and when politely guided, they almost always fall into agreement when a well phrased starting permission question is posed... e.g.:

'John, it's great to be here with you today. Would it be ok if I outline how I have prepared for this meeting and the order I'd suggest we approach things to best help you?'

Now, even if the prospect is a wise old owl, schooled in the art of sales meetings, there is going to be a *human* element at play here: common courtesy!

Very few professional business people will be rude enough to say, 'Thanks for the offer, but I'd rather be obstructive and insist you adapt on the fly to my own pre-set approach.'

The worst you are likely to get is a clarification on time available, and perhaps a request to include something additional once you have outlined your intention.

It's wise to always conclude your suggested agenda with the question, 'Is there anything else you will need me to address that will enable you make a positive decision?' This is a catchall question that makes sure you don't miss out on anything that's important to them.

Hopefully, all of this positioning will be confirmation in any case, as I'd always suggest setting this intention within your meeting confirmation email or calling ahead of the day itself. That is, this has already been outlined as a suggestion, and they have already had the chance to advise of any different requirement well ahead of the meeting itself. Your positioning statement will have been used at that stage and again at this point. By doing so, you are double checking the prospect's agreement and consent before you then chair that meeting and steer it.

QUESTION SEQUENCING

'If you say it, they'll raise an objection, but if they say it, it's true.'

This quote comes from the great sales legend that is Jeffrey Gitomer (author of several books including *The Sales Bible*).

That quote neatly summarises the value of sales questions. If you find that you are doing most of the talking, it's likely you'll lose. If you are asking insightful, considered, open questions, it's much more likely you'll learn what you need to win more often.

Open questions start with 'what?', 'when?', 'where?', 'who?', and 'why?'.

They also work well with 'how?'

All of these questions require an answer that goes beyond 'yes' or 'no'. They are information gatherers, and they give you all the information you need to get the client's 'truth' from them.

The more open questions play a part in the enquiry handling and fact finding phases of your sales process, the more empowered you will be later on.

Once you have all the information, and you are then presenting your solution, you can still use this information powerfully using reflection and closed confirmation questions, e.g.:

> **YOU** 'Sarah, a little earlier on you explained that not taking sufficient breaks from work often left you feeling very tired and burnt out. How important to you is it to you to make sure that doesn't happen this year?'

> **PROSPECT** 'It's really important, I couldn't face another year without a proper break somewhere sunny.'

> **YOU** 'Ok, that sounds pretty essential then, doesn't it?'

> **PROSPECT** 'Yes, absolutely vital I'd say.'

This short conversation shows how the customer can tell themselves how vital a decision is, without you needing to do anything more than reflect what you heard the first time, and expand a little upon it, before confirming it with a closed question.

Whilst every sales setting does vary a little, and certainly the duration and volume of questions can change massively, the sequencing of those questions is fairly consistent.

Here is the pattern that most commonly arises:

Initial enquiry fact finding questions – Establish the situation of the prospect and their self-perceived *apparent* need.

Expansion questions – Clarification on the true needs, and investigation into core customer motives (pains and gains).

Need reflection questions – Questions that reflect your understanding and allow the customer to confirm their position, expectations, wishes, and required outcomes.

Pre-closing questions – These are questions designed to establish the client's readiness and capability to buy now. They may relate to budget, other decision makers, delivery date expectations, or a range of other factors.

Solution based questions – Questions that allow you to filter the customer towards a decision. These are based on known solutions, and now matching customer preferences.

Confirmation and progression questions – These questions are designed to get the customer to verbally confirm their requirements and that the solution meets their needs, and to gain permission to proceed with an order.

As an exercise, it's worth writing out a set of questions for each area, so that you start to develop your brain's 'muscle memory'. This is when you don't have to think too much before you ask the right question, and building up the bank helps a lot.

By having a set of default and easy-to-use questions

available, your application will become less 'consciously competent' and more automated.

The more natural you can become in your sales conversation, even within the framework detailed above, the better your success rate will be.

Sales systemisation

Earlier in the book I explained a bit about swim-lane mapping and how it can be applied to sales systemisation – the main point being that whilst sales people will always have their uniqueness, the company's approach to sales should be consistent.

By insisting that the steps are mapped out, and encouraging all team members to input on what those steps should be and how they should be completed, we get closer to the desired nirvana.

The nirvana being a system that, when followed by anyone with the required competence in selling, delivers a consistent and reasonably predictable output. Three prospects results in one customer. Average value sale to be achieved is £X. This consistency of approach, and foreseeability of results, makes business growth forecasting much more valuable to the business as it actually starts to look and feel realistic.

One thing to realise is that sales people tend to be quite dynamic, and systemisation is not always natural to them. This is why it is vital to engage with them early, encourage sharing of what is working and what isn't, and to base the current sales approach and system on the best known actions and results achieved. It is hard to argue that you have a better way without having the metrics to back it up.

It's also hard to refine and improve sales results when all the processes are altered simultaneously; it's better to identify a likely point of improvement, make the change, test and measure the outcome, and then either adopt it longer term or make a different change. Proceed one change at a time, sequentially, adopting changes according to the result improvements that are proven, not suspected.

SALES TOOLKITS

Within the sales process stages, there will be a need to develop relevant and timely tools to support the team in completing their activities well.

This might be the provision of simple assets such as professional business cards, brochures or videos, or it may extend into such things as buyer guides, presentations, or access to resources (such as demonstration vehicles for test drives in the earlier example).

Failing to provide these tools, or relying on the sales people to design them independently, will often lead to inconsistency of approach and of results. It also will often lead to an inconsistency of prospect experience between the marketing contacts and the sales contacts.

When you review the sales map that is created for your company or for a particular service or product, it's likely that an audit of all existing sales support tools will bring up several versions that have been gradually adapted or personalised by the sales team. Having an open discussion over these changes, the benefits they have brought, and the thinking behind them can often yield some very interesting and helpful input for the final 'drawn together' version that is then agreed for adoption by all members moving forward.

Chapter 9 - Reflection and Exercise

We have a systemised sales process for all core services/product groups? **YES / NO**

The core objection handlers (derailers and hesitators) have been documented, shared, and updated recently? **YES / NO**

We have undertaken recent and up-to-date sales training to improve our skillsets in that department? **YES / NO**

I believe that our sales systems, processes, and tools are optimised and delivering the best results possible for the business? **YES / NO**

IF NO:

I believe that these can be enhanced in the following areas and ways...

....

....

....

....

Team members who should be involved in that refinement process are:

....

....

....

....

Chapter 10

KPIs AND GAUGES

Have you ever spent a night or two as a patient in hospital? If so, it's likely that you will have experienced the joy of being connected, via a maze of wiring, to a number of monitors.

You may well have even been lucky enough to have a screen adjacent to your bed that had a range of numbers, graphs, and other icons denoting your critical health information: blood pressure, oxygen saturation levels, heart rate, and so on.

These metrics were monitored to ensure that you were kept in good health and to help flag when something was inconsistent with expectations.

Heart stops or starts beating rapidly... warning bells and whistles.

Oxygen saturation starts to decline... warning bells and whistles.

...and so on.

Now these metrics weren't just monitored passively awaiting those crisis moments. There is normally a regular check in by a nurse or doctor to take readings and identify trends that happen over the longer periods of time.

This is done so that they can identify improvement or decline against a desired projection.

What does this have to do with business?

All of the metrics mentioned above are critical to human health and wellbeing. In the same way, your business has some vital signs, and you need to be aware of them and react to them accordingly.

Each function in the business (operations, marketing, sales, personnel, financials, R&D) has indicators that show how it is performing.

Now in most business books you will have read or learned about KPIs (key performance indicators). These are the metrics that show an outcome:

➤ Number of enquiries

➤ Number of clients

➤ Turnover

➤ Gross Profit

➤ Net Profit

➤ Units produced

➤ Hours billed

...and many more; these are all outcome KPIs.

What you are less likely to have seen is reference to KPAs (key performance activities). These are the driving metrics that generate the KPIs.

This is an important distinction as in many cases, businesses focus in on a KPI and the desire for it to change, but don't actually identify the relevant KPAs. If they did, they would then focus mostly on the targeting of KPAs, and then the results would change more.

As an example, I can stare at the number of enquiries my business is receiving each month and hope for a change. I might even go and issue an instruction to my marketing team that I want to see enquiry levels increase.

But if I haven't identified the KPAs that are causing the current results, all I am doing is pointing out a problem and shouting that I wish it were different.

Imagine going to the doctor and saying, 'My foot hurts, but I wish it didn't,' and the doctor says, 'Yes, I wish that too,' before leaving the room and taking no action. They return a week later and say, 'How's your foot?' and you say, 'Still broken.'

It would be madness, wouldn't it?

If you spot the symptom of a problem (an outcome KPI that isn't where you want and believe it should be), then the logical way forward is to investigate the inputs (the KPAs) and either change the method of delivery (through the system or the person) or change the volume of activity.

The key question to be asking is always, 'Is this a system problem or a person problem?' In other words, are we not doing the right things, or are they not being completed effectively?

A simple example might be as follows:

Input KPA – the number of telemarketing calls made

Output KPI – the number of meetings booked with qualified prospects

If the output KPI is too low, then the input KPA needs investigating.

If the KPA level appears to be ok, then we need to investigate the effectiveness of that activity and potentially review or refine the telemarketing system, it's procedures, and/or its tools. This might require some further, more detailed metrics to be established and tested against.

If the KPA level appears low, then we need to investigate that. Is the telephone equipment working ok? Has the person been training sufficiently? Is there a motivation issue? Only by reviewing the potential causes can we then seek to adapt the KPA moving forward.

It's a simple approach, but it works well. In the same way as a mechanic diagnoses issues in an engine, we are investigating our business and working on corrective repairs.

MANAGING BUSINESS KPIs

There are potentially a *lot* of numbers in a business. If you really put your mind to it, I bet you could find a hundred things to measure for each function within the company. A hundred for marketing, a hundred for sales, a hundred for operations, and so on.

However, the issue then becomes measuring for measurement's sake, or put another way, paralysis by analysis.

That's why you need to identify the headline numbers for the top tier, and then the performance metrics for each department, team, and individual.

The individuals record and report to the managers.

The managers collate and report to the directors.

The directors collate and report to the CEO/owners.

It's an upward reporting system.

That's an important point. It is an *upward* system. The numbers are recorded and reported at one level, and then reported in a required format and to a required timeframe to the level above.

This activity is a performance standard for that role. It isn't a nice to have, and it certainly shouldn't need 'downward chasing'.

Each team member is clear on their role and what they need to report, how, and when.

Each manager understands what is due and when. They also understand what they need to collate and what is required for them to report upwards, how, and when.

...and so on for every team, to every department head, to every director, to the owner.

By following this relatively simple upward flow of information, the business leaders should not have to request information downwards other than in one specific situation... one of the numbers either isn't clear or isn't where it needs to be from a goal perspective.

How to make it happen

The key to this approach is to have a really clear organisational chart (by role). Once you are clear on where your people have responsibilities, you can start to assign recording and reporting duties.

This should include a clear instruction on the how (what the report will look like and include) and when (at what time, date, and frequency the report is required).

An organisational chart (by role) is different to a traditional organisation chart (by name). Where a traditional organisational chart will only have a person's name included once (normally against the highest role they occupy), the organisational chart by role may have their name shown in several positions.

This is because in most SME businesses (and unlike some larger corporates), staff members may carry one title for the purpose of their business card and email signature but in reality be wearing the hats of five or more jobs.

They may well be Operations Director, but they are also Operations Admin Clerk, Warehouse Manager, and Marketing Apprentice. Each of the roles they fulfil have duties, responsibilities, and metrics to report to show that they are performing to standard (or not).

As an example, below are the organisational charts for my coaching business.

The first shows us by name, and the second shows us by roles. What is immediately obvious is that there are many more roles than people!

When we look at the name-based version, it's easy to see how we might forget what needs to be tracked or reported, but when we see it by roles, it becomes more obvious how the data for different roles and different departments would come together for the leadership team.

Name-based organisational chart

Only shows the number of people, and their most senior title.

Names in red are not employed directly by the business (i.e. supply to).

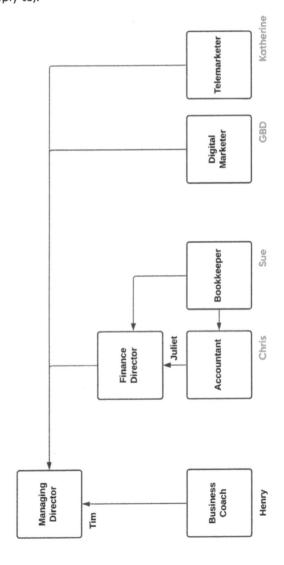

Role-based organisational chart

Shows the number of true roles and who is fulfilling them.

Names in red are not employed directly by the business (i.e. supply to).

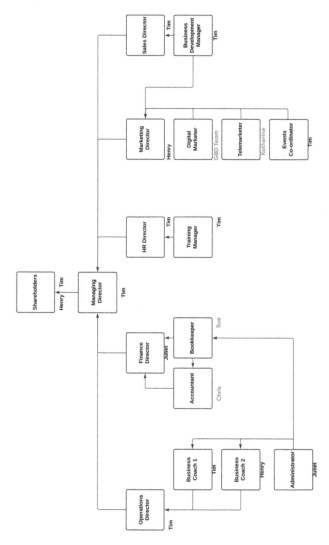

The important element to spot here is that *every* role should have some performance metrics to report upon, and the line manager above should receive these clearly and consistently.

This upward cycling of information is a requirement from each team member, and what they are reporting depends on the role that they are fulfilling. If they have multiple hats, that means multiple reports, but they are all cleanly separated out to the related function.

A fantastic resource that addresses this upward (submarine) style of management is by L. David Marquet.

Reference: *Turn the Ship Around! A True Story of Turning Followers Into Leaders* – Book by L. David Marquet

The book is based on the real story of a genuine nuclear submarine commander and how great efficiency and effectiveness gains were made by adopting this revolutionary approach.

General points on Metrics and Gauges

I have already covered what metrics you should be looking for in your business:

➤ The essential output KPIs

➤ The critical driver KPAs

What I haven't done is define exactly how many there should be for your business, and that's been intentional.

Not every business is the same, and perhaps importantly, not every business owner or manager is the same. Crucially, not every business has the same objectives.

Whilst there are likely to be a number of common measurements desired for almost all companies (perhaps those relating to profit levers and financial control), there also needs to be a degree of flexibility here.

As a coach, I have spoken with many business owners over the years who feel they are told to measure a specific list of things that are either genuinely irrelevant or for which they have not yet connected the dots between the what and the why.

By taking the approach of defining the desired outcomes you want to achieve for your business first and then working back to the KPAs that drive those, this typically dull and logistics-focused task can actually become more interesting and more motivating.

In fact, the profit levers model I explained earlier was born of this thinking. I simply asked myself, 'What is the overall company profit dependent upon?' That led to the breakdown shown in the model, and then the subsets of that, and eventually led to the strategic areas that contributed through KPAs and the smaller dependency KPIs.

For your own business, I recommend an 'outcome first' approach to creating your relevant KPIs, KPAs, and then the gauges (dashboards) to display them upon.

Start with the core outcome you want to achieve for the business or department

(ultimate summary KPI, e.g. overall profit)

Identify the dependency KPIs – the ones that combine to deliver the core KPI

(e.g. individual revenue stream profits)

Identify the KPAs that will drive those dependency KPIs

(The activities that, if completed in higher volumes or to better effect, change the results, e.g. number of sales calls made)

Remember, it's not possible or time-efficient to measure everything, and even if you did, it's unlikely you would have either the time to review it or the resources to respond to those results. The aim here is not a microscopic evaluation of every facet of the business, but sufficient 'flagging' to notify when goals are on track and when control measures are within tolerances. This is why RAG (red/amber/green) tagging within your reports is so often the simplest but most effective method of quickly flagging issues:

Green = ahead of schedule, above target, fully completed, and so on.

Amber = on track, on target, and so on

Red = behind schedule, below target, and so on.

As human beings we are highly visual creatures, and our assessment of danger is fast. Having a report (or set of reports) that can be quickly scanned and risks identified is very powerful for enabling response.

I have mentioned several times the value of technology, and as your business scales up, the accessibility (in financial terms) of automated recording, reporting, and even first stage reacting tools is becoming more and more available.

There are now fire alarm systems that can identify issues and automatically extinguish... and the equivalent is available for a wide range of business functions, across almost all industry sectors.

For training companies, learning management systems can show which students attended, who completed the homework, who passed the exams, and how many times they took them.

It is amazing how the world is moving forward, and my recommendation is to speak with the software companies that have sprung up to support almost all business types. Some of these are generic, but there also many that are industry-specific.

Check them out; there is a huge amount of leverage, efficiency gain, and response-ability available through the adoption of relevant technology.

Chapter 10 – Reflection and Exercise

Use these grids to note the vital numbers for your business.

You can add more rows on a spreadsheet for others if you want to.

Remember that KPIs are the output (result) number and the KPAs are the input numbers (the drivers).

Our Top 2 OPERATIONAL KPIs are...	The Driving KPAs for this are...

Our Top 2 MARKETING KPIs are...	The Driving KPAs for this are...

Our Top 2 SALES KPIs are...	The Driving KPAs for this are...

Our Top 2 FINANCIAL KPIs are...	The Driving KPAs for this are...

Our Top 2 HR KPIs are...	The Driving KPAs for this are...

SYSTEMISE FOR EFFICIENCY

Whilst explaining sales mapping earlier, I shared the concept of system mapping.

This approach is really valuable for any system that is either complex or involves many stages, and I will share a few pointers for making it work well within your business here.

First, let's look at the component parts...

➤ A system is a set of processes, connected together in a 'map' (see opposite).

➤ A process is an individual stage within that system, for example:

➤ A procedure is the hidden detail behind each

> **Provides customer with info pack for stated needs**

process. These are detailed 'how to' guides that explain all the individual steps and actions within each process.

Here is an example procedure for providing the customer with information relating to their needs:

Procedure for providing client with information

Once the customer has been seated and provided

For example, this is a map for 'Initial enquiry management – customer showroom visit':

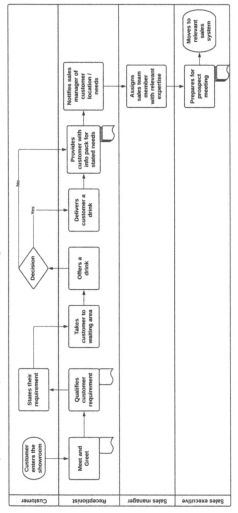

- A swim-lane within a system shows the activities to be completed by that role, for example (for the receptionist):

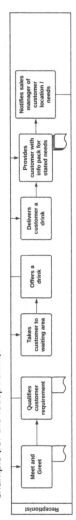

with a drink (if desired),

1. Visit the company information stands by the sales desks.

2. Collect the specific brochure relating to the customer enquiry (if a sales prospect)

AND/OR

our vehicle repair service (if the customer is visiting for a vehicle repair, service, or MOT)

AND/OR

If the visit is for any other reason, print the Wifi code which is stored on the reception desk computer desktop – a document marked 'Wifi password'.

➤ A tool is any asset that is required for the successful completion of the procedure or is supportive of that outcome, for example:

In this example procedure, the brochures, Wifi code, and documents about servicing, repairs, and other items are all

> **Provides customer with info pack for stated needs**

'Tools'. You can see these indicated on the bottom right of the procedure (in this case as a 'multiple document' symbol as it covers a range of options and materials).

I appreciate that these examples are very simple, and were

this to be for a real business, we may choose to combine a few of the separate processes (and procedures) together.

In the example I have separated the processes visually to show the stages more clearly, but in reality the skill is in minimising the number of required process steps within a system, *without* making any individual procedure overly lengthy. This is to help team members remember each process and the related procedural actions more easily. In my experience, a procedure is too long if an experienced member of the team cannot easily remember it and write it out again simply.

One important guideline for creating procedures is that they should not (ideally) reference more than one role at a time. This is not including the customer (or other external stakeholder, e.g. supplier).

The reason for this is fairly obvious: as human beings we are naturally most interested in the parts of a procedure that involve us and are less interested in those that our colleagues are responsible for. There is a tendency for procedures that have multiple roles involved to be 'scan-read' rather than 'detail-read', and this often results in a step or two being unconsciously missed out. This is not a hard and fast rule – there will be occasions where a number of people will be involved in activities all at once – but wherever possible, my advice would be to adopt the KIS approach of 'Keep It Simple'.

Another point worth noting is that each time a progress arrow crosses a swim-lane border, there is a need for communication between parties. In simple terms, the golden principle is to create confirmations at the end of each procedure:

➤ a communication from the person completing the first procedure that they have done so, and informing the next person in the chain that they are now due to pick up that baton (next sequential activity);

➤ confirmation from the second role holder back to the first that they have received that communication and will be undertaking the next activities.

Depending on the setting, this might be as simple as a short conversation happening, or in more complex stages it may require a handover checklist and sign off.

When I was a police officer, we used a 'chain of evidence' mindset for any exhibits or tasks that needed to move from person to person in the course of an investigation.

It was essential that whenever this happened, we either signed a document, file, or evidence bag to show the time of handover, who it went from and to, and various other elements depending on the setting. This wasn't a 'nice to have' but more a case of 'you may well get fired or lose a case if you don't'.

It mattered, and everyone knew it. For that reason, there were very limited occasions where it ever didn't happen!

For your own business systems, processes, and procedures, you will have to decide on the level of expectation, training, and compliance requirement you place upon your team and suppliers, but I have personally always leaned quite heavily on these points for compliance.

This, I guess, is partly my background and own training, but also comes as a result of experience in various businesses. In short, I have found that we rarely go to the effort of creating these robust systems, processes, and detailed procedures for activities in a business that don't really matter. We build them, train them, and adopt them because the outcomes of those activities are known to be important and often will change the performance of people and the business as a whole.

For this reason, it's essential that when you build these forms of systems and all the elements within them, you are doing it for the aspects that are less flexible – the parts you *really* want it done 'that way and that way only'.

If there is flexibility, then build it in and make it obvious – e.g. 'greet the customer courteously' rather than 'say these exact words'.

Getting that balance right will show that you trust your team and that you are all only building the system compliance aspects rigidly where it truly matters, and not for the purpose of being an unyielding despot!

SYSTEM OVERVIEW DIRECTORY

Within this section I have shown you how you can create system maps for a set of related processes and for a particular phase within a company – to get you from one point to another point, as part of a sequence of smaller systems that together form a larger journey.

It isn't the whole customer experience in one map, and it certainly doesn't cover all the behind the scenes elements that take place within a business.

Understanding and creating the index for your system directory is really useful for making it easy for you and your staff to locate, follow, and update the business systems manual.

I have seen many different ways of doing this, from simple printed folders to highly refined intranet systems. Whichever you choose, you'll need to segment the systems into groups with a logical 'hierarchy tree' to help quickly recognise and filter down to the required detail. It is well worth having a chat with a systems consultant if you want to take this part of business improvement to the ultimate. ISO accreditations and others all exist to help companies create systems and ensure they are compliantly and effectively followed.

Each business has different stages, but they normally separate into the following elements:

➤ **Systems that happen before dealing with a customer** (e.g. supplier selection)

➤ **Systems that happen whilst dealing with a customer** (e.g. any marketing & sales contact, order processing, payments, etc.)

➤ **Systems that happen after dealing with a customer** (e.g. actions that depend upon their selections and experiences)

AND

➤ **Systems that are separate from client interactions** (e.g. many of the topics that are within the coaching star above plus a few more, such as procurement)

Here is an example of some items that might go into a systems list

(there will be many more – these are just idea starters for you!)

Examples of Systems for SMEs	
Office + Administration	IT hardware systems – efficient and safe IT software systems – cost efficient and suited to tasks General (opening, closing, alarms, machinery etc)
Finance	Book Keeping Payroll Tax Planning (VAT, Corporation, Income / other) Management Accounts (reports + tracking) Cashflow forecasting + tracking Debtor management systems + tracking
Marketing	Website maintenance / upgrades CRM (Customer Relationship Management) Marketing automation software Performance tracking systems and software
Sales	Active prospect management systems (CRM / Ecommerce etc) Marketing budget tracking (e.g. PPC / other media) Sales process re-engineering (minimise objections / hesitators)
Operations	Stock management Supply chain management Production management Fulfilment / delivery management Returns / compaints management
HR	Staff handbooks Induction systems Performance management systems Holiday systems Record keeping / information sharing systems Discipline and grievance management systems

Ultimately, there are several methods for systemising your business, and my intention here has not been to steer you too heavily towards the one I am most familiar with. My aim has been more to help you see the opportunity that systems present and also to encourage you to engage in their development.

… Your consistency and an improvement of business results will be connected to this concept!

WHEN IS SYSTEMISATION THE RIGHT SOLUTION?

This is an interesting question to ask. In theory, every business should be fully systemised and have a lovely manual of how to do all the repeated tasks.

That's a great theory.

Practically speaking, however, creating a systems manual is a big undertaking. This is particularly true if you have an established business and yet didn't start the task at the outset.

When this is the case, there can be literally hundreds of procedures that should all be documented out and connected into the system and then into the overview map.

It can feel overwhelming as a task, and unless the intention is to create a franchise or other business format where a completely written down manual is *essential*, it may be overkill to attempt at this point in your business.

Taking a look back at our Business Star model, you can see that there are three 'tiers' of progression:

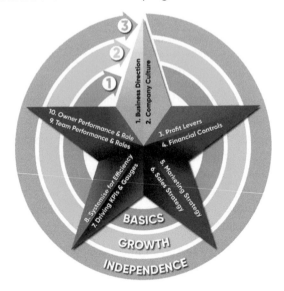

When you consider these in the context of systemisation levels, it's easy to think as follows:

BASICS:

Simple workflows and key outcome metrics for all repeated and core tasks.

Checklists applied and used to ensure systems are followed where relevant.

The aim is to enable consistency of approach, and to provide a performance basis for 'how the work should be done' for all staff.

GROWTH:

Advance the workflows into system maps and defined processes that align with the defined organisational roles.

Review and refine the systems, processes, and procedures regularly to ensure they are still fit for purpose, and periodically when performance improvement is sought against an existing approach.

Checklists still used to ensure systems are followed where relevant.

Procedures are clearly recorded and provide a solid reference for staff to remind themselves of the current methods, and as a performance management resource.

INDEPENDENCE:

Systems to be advanced to the point where a new staff member for any role can easily and quickly follow the instructions and complete the tasks to the same outcomes as the existing team.

Business owner tasks to be systemised and, where possible, devolved to employed staff also. Reduce reliance and enable independence.

Summary

The key issue I am raising here is that whilst many books will guide you to systemise fully just as a general principle that is good for busines, there is a time and a place to reach that zenith. Work out the objective that is relevant to you right now, and work the systems up to that level in the most efficient way possible. When you are ready for the next step, advance from there.

Basics = functional

Growth = efficient and improving

Independence = allowing autonomy and exit

Chapter 11 – Reflection and Exercise

Use this document to create a current systems audit. Once done, you will be more able to plan, as you can identify where the priorities for systemisation exist and what the next progression stage is to.

FINANCIAL SYSTEMS	Basic	Growth	Independence
e.g. invoicing system		✓	
MARKETING SYSTEMS			
SALES SYSTEMS			
OPERATIONAL SYSTEMS			
HR SYSTEMS			
ADMIN & OTHER SYSTEMS			

Chapter 12

TEAM PERFORMANCE AND ROLES

First things first – be clear on the roles, and help your team be that way too!

In Chapter 10, we spoke about 'role-based' organisational charts, where we separate out the roles within a business and assign them individually to the personnel.

By doing so, you will recall, it becomes easier to spot *all* the responsibilities that exist within a company and to ensure that no matter what the 'title' an employee may carry, the sub-roles are not omitted.

The way this works best is to take a look at the full role-based organisational chart and to match up all existing staff with the roles that they actually fulfil... whether or not *you or they* yet realise that's what they are doing!

It is almost universal that when business owners take a look at the jobs that are really being done, versus those that are perceived as being done, there is a gap or a misunderstanding... and it doesn't matter whether that is a misunderstanding for the employer, the manager, or the team member.

It's a problem when it happens.

As an example – Bob, the 'Deliveries Manager' actually has three roles:

Deliveries Manager – the primary job title Bob has

Warehouse Operative – a secondary role that Bob undertakes

Administrator – a tertiary role that Bob undertakes

These roles may look like this in the organisational chart:

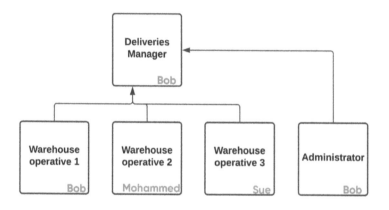

As you can see, the three roles are individually identified within this section of the organisational chart, and other team members are also identified.

Each role within the organisational chart will have key responsibilities, and performance criteria that are expected to be delivered upon.

By having this separation for any substantive grouped set of responsibilities (i.e. each 'role'), it becomes much easier to separate out a set and hire an appropriate new member of the team to take on the emerging role as the scale of responsibilities grows in line with a company's needs.

As an example, if we take the three roles currently fulfilled by Bob, it might be that they break down as follows each week:

Deliveries Manager – 24 hours

Warehouse Operative – 10 hours

Administrator – 11 hours

A total of 35 hours

At the current level, this is manageable during a standard working pattern (9–5 Monday to Friday).

However, as the company grows, the roles start to expand, and Bob and his supervisors soon start to see that overload is happening (or will soon) if additional support isn't provided.

Upon review, the new situation shows the following:

Deliveries Manager – 28 hours

Warehouse Operative – 14 hours

Administrator – 16 hours

A total of 48 hours

This is currently only being achieved by Bob 'overworking', which is stressing him, and through the support of his team, who are also feeling stressed now.

The most complex and specialised skilled tasks that Bob is undertaking are his duties as Deliveries Manager and as the Warehouse Operative. These are the ones that would be most costly to hire additional resource to fulfil.

As such, the business decides to hire a part time administrator to free up Bob (and his colleagues) and enable them to fulfil their duties as Deliveries Manager and Warehouse Operatives without the additional admin responsibilities they used to be responsible for directly.

This is both a cost effective solution and one that is quick to implement due to the simplicity of taking the 'Duties and Responsibilities' section relating to 'Administrator' from within Bob's employment documents and simply creating a new position based upon it.

Here is how that would work:

Team Member: Bob	Job Title: Deliveries Manager
Role 1: Deliveries Manager	
Key responsibilities of Delivery manager	
1.	
2.	
3.	
Role 2: Warehouse Operative	
Key responsibilities of Warehouse Operative	
1.	
2.	
3.	
Role 3: Administrator (THIS SECTION IS SIMPLY RE-ASSIGNED)	
Key responsibilities of Administrator	
1.	
2.	
3.	

This is a very simple method of helping manage the natural growth of duties that happens when a company expands, and the separation of the sub-roles within the job descriptions for each team member makes it quite straight-forward to separate out the tasks that will be devolved to different team members.

It isn't always that simple, but it is certainly *easier* than having one long, unfiltered list of duties for each team member who is in reality not doing one full time job but several roles that together create a full time requirement.

MANAGEMENT OF PERFORMANCE

This is a *huge* topic, and I am only going to skim the surface here.

I will, however, in doing so, share my top tips, learnings, and recommendations for helping your colleagues perform.

Let's start with the formula:

$$\text{Current Performance} = \text{Potential} - \text{Interferences}$$

This fantastic concept comes from *The Inner Game of Tennis* by Timothy Gallwey and really neatly covers a range of issues.

In simple terms, it is saying that the current performance of an individual is the sum of two factors:

Their potential: which is substantial in most cases

Their interferences: everything that is limiting, curtailing, or truncating. This might be a result of lacking the necessary skills, confidence, or motivation or of suffering from fear, over-confidence, relationship or communication issues, or a distorted perception.

When we look at this in the context of employment, the default for many managers is to assume that their colleagues' capability is somehow being reached already. The challenge is actually more often in being able to identify and help them remove the interference that is creating a glass ceiling.

The importance of performance measurement and review

In this book we have already mentioned a concept called 'Submarine management'.

As a quick reminder, this approach is all about the flow of critical information happening in a pro-active upward fashion. The most junior team member reports to their supervisor, who reports upwards, and so on until the combined and shortlisted vital information is clear to those at the top.

This is different (in my experience) to the majority of SME settings, where directors often have to seek information from managers, who then seek it from their direct reports, and so on – top to bottom.

The bottom to top approach provides more personal accountability, responsibility, and efficiency. It also has the advantage that the person who is reporting is the person who is most closely associated with the aspect under review. The person at the coal face is saying what they are seeing and understanding directly, rather than this being done by someone less familiar with the direct situation.

An example of this benefit may be where an engineer has more up to date experience than the supervisor who is less proficient and familiar with new machinery.

To achieve this type of reporting, there are a few factors to consider:

1. What are the responsibilities for the individual, and how is their personal performance to be assessed?

2. What are their responsibilities in terms of reporting their situation and contribution to team/department metrics?

3. What are the manager's responsibilities for collating the individual reports and shortlisting the important summary information for upward and onward communication?

SOME TOP TIPS

Every business needs to provide staff members with a contract of employment (by law in fact).

This document serves a useful purpose in that it sets out the terms and conditions of employment, remuneration, holiday entitlement, and so on. It has a purpose, but often doesn't actually contain much information about what is expected from the individual in terms of performance.

Some will also contain a clear job description, which lists out the various tasks and duties of the employee and often will describe the performance expectation in broad terms – e.g. 'provide the company directors with regular reports on the department's performance'.

This document is again helpful, as in broad terms it outlines what the role involves and what the expectations are in pure language terms. What it often misses are the actual performance measurements or precise expectations. This isn't entirely a bad thing, as if it were to be too precise at this stage it would only be able to define the *minimum* standards required to avoid getting dismissed.

Which is why we need each team member to have a personal development plan.

Because we don't want team members who do just enough to avoid getting fired, we *really want* team members who are constantly striving for self-improvement aligned to the requirements of the company.

We want staff who make 'discretionary effort' and seek to be their best, not just average... and that takes good management and inspirational leadership.

To clarify the difference between management and leadership:

I'll preface my view here by saying that this topic has been debated at the highest levels for decades.

There are definitions galore of what leadership is and what management is. Some are great, many are confusing, and most aren't actually very helpful in a practical sense. Here is my personal take on this thorny topic...

Firstly, managers are by default leaders also. They may not be doing so at a company strategic level, but in many ways their contribution is more vital still as it has more direct and day-to-day influence on the team members.

Effective management includes the traits of effective leadership within the parameters of their influence.

Management = ensuring performance to the standard

This short and snappy definition is saying that at any moment in time, there should be a defined set of performance standards for each team member. There should also be some targets and goals for each team.

The manager is responsible for ensuring that the team members are contributing at the required level for the individual roles they fulfil and also to the collaborative outcomes of the team to which they belong.

The skillset they employ to draw those performance levels up to standard – and to motivate performance that goes above and beyond the baseline to deliver on the targets for the team – will be broad, and certainly more than I want to go into within this book as my aim is to cover a wide range of business areas with top tips, and allow you to complement those ideas and concepts with the detailed support methodologies available within other resources on those specific topics.

So, if you can see the value in 'getting better' on this area of your own business, then go and read a book on effective management and inspirational leadership to give you more knowledge and competence on that specific requirement... or give me a call and ask me to be your coach! J

Managers have the toughest job of all in my view. They have the duty to get the team performing and through that, deliver on the ever-increasing expectations of their own managers or directors. They are the critical hub that makes a business sing. It's a dance of instruction, support, training, accountability, disciplining, motivating, and guiding. They are as skilled as an orchestra conductor who can play 10 instruments well. Don't underappreciate your managers!

Leadership = moving up the levels

For this definition we are talking about business leaders who are heading the team. This can be as a company owner, a director, or as a manager. When you are fulfilling this role, you are the beacon to draw the team onwards and the energy boost that fills their veins with fire.

Great leaders are intrinsically connected with the business purpose. They are the living, breathing embodiment of that inspiring vision for the future. The role of the leader is to make that purpose practical, achievable, and real in the day to day.

Leaders are always looking at the best ways to advance towards that business vision, how to expedite it, and how to deliver above expectation. They are strategic, but they are also the cheerleader for the business and all who work in it.

Now, it's important to say that most leaders are also managers. They have areas of responsibility that are also directly involved with the day-to-day running of the company.

This can often cause confusion about their approach, as leaders don't think about themselves as managers in the same way as managers don't often think about themselves as leaders. The reality in an SME business is that the multi-hat role held by most is an overlap position. There are often direct duties, management duties, and leadership duties that all need to be undertaken by the owner. For that reason, I don't like to separate out their title as leader or manager, but in the same way as in a small hospital, a surgeon sometimes does the tasks of a nurse or a porter, the skillset and work of the business owner can be varied.

What I *can* tell you is that the best leaders are not aloof. When needed, they get down in the trenches and fight alongside their team... and they don't expect or need to be thanked for that.

As a real-world example of this, I'll refer back to my days as a young police officer in Brighton. At the time I was leading a small team of probationary officers (early stage of service and under mentorship).

On one afternoon, a mini-riot began in the Whitehawk housing estate.

For those who don't know the area, Whitehawk is on the east side of Brighton and had a bit of a 'reputation' for trouble. It would be fair to say that a proportion of the residents were actively hostile to police presence, and it was not uncommon for violence to occur towards officers on patrol in the area.

On this particular day, a thief had been apprehended by a police officer on duty and had resisted arrest. When support officers arrived to assist the individual officer, many residents had also come out from their properties to support their friend. This had escalated quickly into a stand-off between the police and a fairly large crowd (perhaps 100 in total).

I had been called on the radio to attend and had taken my team up to the location. We had established a line of officers to create a cordon between the person under arrest and the crowd who wished for him to be set free. The situation was volatile, and a fair few choice words were being shared with my colleagues by some of the less friendly locals!

Whilst my colleagues were doing their best to subdue the prisoner, and to manage a number of others who had also offended in one way or another, it was taking a few minutes and tensions were rising.

First it was words being thrown, and then it was stones, then bottles.

Whilst a few small shields were available in the immediate vehicles at the site, and were quickly put to use to defend ourselves, none of us was equipped with full PPE (personal protective equipment), helmets, or riot gear. There were perhaps 15 officers and 100 in the crowd. The odds were not in our favour!

It was at this stage that two really fantastic pieces of leadership came about.

The first was a brave decision by the operational commander, who was located a few miles away back in the control room. Their decision was brave because it involved doing the precise opposite of what would have been obvious. They did not send lots of officers to the scene to join in.

What they did was assess the situation calmly and come up with a plan that met the purpose of the police; they worked out how to de-escalate the situation, create safety for all, and enable the offenders to be dealt with.

Here is what they did.

They quickly realised that the location was well covered by CCTV with a recording capability. They also identified that whilst it might be possible to co-ordinate a full out assault by police forces on the area, that wasn't the most effective option. Instead, they created a fleet of vehicles to attend the scene and quickly remove the immediate offenders (those under arrest already) and the current officers from the area. They had recognised that the focus of the hate was not properties or public, but the police. Whilst they were performing their duties, they were the focal point for the anger. Remove the fuel, and the flames die down.

This was a brave call. There are those who at that time believed it was weak to act in this way. It didn't show the 'fist' of the long arm of the law.

My view, and I think the view of most now, is that it was inspired leadership. It worked beautifully. The fleet of police vehicles went in convoy to the location on blue lights and two tone sirens. Upon arrival, all officers and all current prisoners were loaded quickly, and then, to the total surprise of the baying mob, it simply drove away at speed. Leaving a crowd with no focus for their anger.

Within a few minutes, normality had returned.

Now, you might say that is weak; they ran away!

Not at all. You see, at about 4am the next morning, and over the following few days as more of the offenders in the crowd were identified from the high quality CCTV footage, a set of arrests were made. Officers attended the homes of the known offenders and arrested them calmly, and on their terms.

No crowds, limited resistance. Beautiful!

Within the space of a few days, this operation had changed from a violent riot with potential for hundreds of injuries or worse into an object lesson that bad behaviour now can lead to a timely comeuppance later.

It still remains one of the best pieces of practical police leadership I saw whilst on the front lines.

I did mention that there were two pieces of leadership. That was the first.

The second was simple. The vehicles that arrived to collect the officers from the scene were not driven just by the regular front line staff.

There were custody Sergeants, Inspectors, and even a Superintendent behind the wheel. They had heard the commotion on the radio and had volunteered to drive into that setting and help their colleagues out.

This showed a commitment that went beyond their regular roles (some were mainly office based), and I and my colleagues on the day saw that. It gave us confidence in their leadership, and their commitment. It wasn't about their role at the time but about their commitment to the prevention of crime and the protection of life.

Ways to advance your team's performance

First, it's important that you and they are clear on their roles, their responsibilities, and the expectations. These can be managed well using a variety of standard HR documents including the contract of employment, role description, and role-related KPIs and performance standards.

Second, whilst the role and the performance standards might be set from the outset, your team are not static. Their performance can move up, and it can also move down. The way in which you plan, deliver, and review training and skills will play a part, but so too will the regularity and methods of communication you employ.

Within his book *The Rockerfeller Habits*, Verne Harnish refers to what he calls the 'rhythm' of meetings.

This is simply the frequency, format, and purpose with which meetings are completed with team members. This covers individual meetings, team meetings, and company-wide meetings (in person or online).

Every business will be slightly different, and certainly the location basis, regional or international structure, and so on will affect how these sessions are run.

The core ethos behind the thinking doesn't, however.

For the individuals – what frequency and format is sufficient to properly enable their performance, and their passion?

For the team – what frequency and format is sufficient to engage, support, review, and develop?

For the company – what frequency and format is relevant to ensure alignment, engagement, and inspiration towards the company purpose and goals overall?

Daily huddles, weekly reviews, monthly reports, quarterly planning, annual direction setting, and more. There are many reasons and structures for meetings, but the critical element for me is that they should have a *value* add.

If you are running a meeting, make sure it has a purpose. If it will result in actions, have a record of what the goals, commitments, and review points will be. These need to be added to the participants' diaries, and the managers' for review.

This is important. For many years I attended, and even ran, meetings where those notes weren't made. If they were, they were not applied directly into the system for working, and as a result, the actions were incomplete, late, or not as intended. Now I have the personal habit that I put tasks into my diary and insist my team do likewise during or at the end of the meeting. The same is true for my coaching clients.

It is *much* more productive and makes meetings more accountable, as the next one always starts with an update on actions from the previous.

Chapter 12 – Reflection and Exercise

We have a clear organisational chart by role that shows all the roles and the names of current team members fulfilling them assigned. **YES / NO**

Each team member is clear on ALL the roles that fall under their job title. **YES / NO**

Each role that they fulfil has a detailed and clear explanation of the responsibilities and related performance criteria for those roles. **YES / NO**

Each role has a clear set of reportable metrics, and a specified time and format for presenting those 'up' through the management structure (submarine management system). **YES / NO**

NOTES ON THIS SECTION TO HELP US PROGRESS OUR BUSINESS:

....

....

....

....

....

....

....

....

....

....

Chapter 13

OWNER PERFORMANCE AND ROLES

In Michael Gerber's fantastic book *The E-Myth Revisited*, he talks about three stages to a business owner's development.

The first level is TECHNICIAN

The Technician is the doer.

At this level, the business owner is the job owner too (harking back to Robert Kiyosaki's model also). They are most happy being directly involved and believe that is essential. They often struggle with any delegation, all systems are in their head, and their income is almost directly proportional to the hours applied by them).

The second level is MANAGER

The manager creates order and routines out of chaos.

At this level, the owner is making use of colleagues around them and is starting to delegate and engage, with productivity that goes above the constraints of their own personal and direct input. They are starting to systemise and to enable the knowledge in their head and that of their team to become a fundamental fabric of the business model. The owner is improving productivity but is still very much focused on today, more than tomorrow.

The third tier is ENTREPRENEUR

The Entrepreneur is the visionary.

At this level, the owner may or may not be directly involved in the business tasks of the day. They are highly strategic and are thinking beyond the boundaries of how the work is done, and into the realms of what the possibilities are for the business moving forward. They are planning the growth, the future, and the potential.

> **Quote:** *'While the Manager lives in the past and the Entrepreneur lives in the future, the Technician lives in the present.'*

I haven't explained this precisely as Gerber does within his book, but more as my own interpretation. I am connecting the dots between Kiyosaki's stages of business, my own five stages of business progression and Gerber's three personalities. By doing so, we end up with a joined-up and meaningful avatar for each tier. This is helpful as it plays very much into the three tiers of The Business Star – the basics, growth, and independence.

I wanted to draw all of those concepts together so that you can see the synergy between them, and my thinking for this overarching business development model.

Now, having defined the concept, we also need to make this highly practical for the owner wanting to move from level to level, and the way we do that is to go back to our old friend the organisational chart by role.

We all wear a lot of hats.

Whilst the SME business owner is often only thought of as being as the founder, CEO, MD, or whatever other title they choose to self-bestow, in reality they actually wear many hats (role titles).

It's not uncommon for an SME business owner to in fact have 15 or more roles to fulfil personally – particularly if they are a start-up or only have a small team. Here are some of the many titles they tend to be wearing without realising it clearly:

Shareholder/Owner
Managing Director
Marketing Director

Business Development Manager
Sales Director
Sales Executive
Account Handler

Operations Director
Technician – whatever the 'operations' role is (e.g. plumber)
Head of Research and Development

HR Director
Training Manager

Finance Director
Management Accountant
Bookkeeper
Credit Controller

In the early days of a business (and in some cases for many years), some or all of these roles are achieved almost exclusively by the business owner. Wow!

It's no surprise that most 'business owners' who have not had any formal business skills training can struggle. That's a heck of a CV to have achieved within one's employment history before taking on a company.

Lots learn through trial and error, and lots suffer from the Dunning–Kruger effect because, compared to their peers (who also have had minimal training), they appear to be average (and perceive themselves as better than that!)

Add in the fact that for most business owners who are wearing several hats, they don't have great time management or prioritisation skills, and we can really start to see where the headaches come about.

Don't panic – I have some *great* ideas to share with you on how to make this all a bit more manageable, and how to organise yourself and your day to be more effective and balanced.

Creating a 'Balanced Diary'

First things first.

Run the 'organisational chart by role' exercise for yourself to identify *all* the hats you wear. Put your name next to each.

Second, define the roles and key responsibilities – exactly as you would if you were looking to recruit for that role. Remember that the best job descriptions have all the roles separated out and the aligned responsibilities nice and clear. This is the groundwork you must put in early to prepare. The clearer you make it here, the more defined your diary can ultimately become, and the easier delegation and devolution of roles will be later on.

Third, assess the time and potential for simple systemisation for each role, or the core actions required within it. By doing so, you can start to understand your options for automating, delegating, or retaining it.

Finally, once you have created the framework of roles, core responsibilities, and an approximate frequency and time allowance to ensure no balls are dropped, you can start to create a 'Balanced Diary'.

A balanced diary is no more than a forward planned schedule of activities that is considered against the regular requirements for each role you have a hat for.

It looks rather different to the standard 'appointments diary' that most SME owners are currently operating, in that it shows the roles to be performed during pre-defined timeframes, and only latterly are appointments overlaid.

An example of how a single day in a balanced diary may appear is shown opposite.

This might represent some of the roles to be expected in the balanced diary of the owner of a small construction company.

As you can see, this diary has been set up to contain some of the expected daily and weekly tasks for the business owner.

In this case, on Mondays they have included some daily accounts work under the role of Finance Director, Operations Director, and Managing Director, as well as some weekly tasks under the role of Operations Manager.

One key point to note is that the daily items really should not be moved elsewhere in the week (or even month). They have been decided upon as 'daily tasks' because that is the most appropriate frequency for those tasks to be completed. This might be to prevent build-up of vital tasks, for early identification on critical numbers, or something else, but daily has been decided as being best... so stick to that idea!

	Balance Diary
	Plan for Mondays
09:00 - 09:30	Team meeting
09:30 - 10:00	FINANCIAL DIRECTOR - daily accounts checks
10:00 - 10:30	Travel
10:30 - 11:00	
11:00 - 11:30	
11:30 - 12:00	OPERATIONS MANAGER - site visit 1
12:00 - 12:30	
12:30 - 13:00	
13:00 - 13:30	LUNCH BREAK
13:30 - 14:00	
14:00 - 14:30	
14:30 - 15:00	OPERATIONS DIRECTOR - site visit 1
15:00 - 15:30	
15:30 - 16:00	Travel
16:00 - 16:30	OPERATIONS DIRECTOR - Summary reports
16:30 - 17:00	MANAGING DIRECTOR - Plan tomorrow

These blocks will have been defined by an initial 'time plan', such as is shown below, and then placed into the weekly diary (or perhaps a four-weekly diary) plan to show the regularity of core role responsibilities (annual, quarterly, monthly, weekly, or daily in most cases).

Example of building a time plan:

	TIME BLOCKS REQUIRED (hours)				
	Daily	Weekly	Monthly	Quarterly	Annually
Role: Financial Director					
Start of day review (1 x 0.5 hr)	0.5				
End of week review and reports (1 x 2 hr)		2			
Monthly Summary Reports (1 x 0.5 weekly & 1 x 2 monthly)		0.5	2		
Prepare Director Reports (1 x 1 monthly, 1 x 3 quarterly, 2 x 8 annually)			1	3	16
Role: Bookkeeper					
Regular actions – invoicing, reconciliations etc (5 x 1 hr)	1				
Credit control (2 x 0.5 hr)		1			
Role: Operations Director					
Manage operations team – daily meetings (5 x 0.5)	0.5				
Operations team monthly meeting (1 x 4)			4		
Site visits weekly (4 x 2 hours)		8			
Role: Sales Executive					
Sales meetings – 4 per week (1.5 x 4)		6			
Sales follow ups / account management	0.5				
Lunch breaks (5 x 1 hr)	1				
LINE TOTALS	17.5	17.5			
TOTALS PER WEEK	35				

In this example you can see that the person has four main roles defined, and the tasks that allow them to deliver on their core responsibilities are identified within each. The grid helps this person to define the required frequency for tasks and then to apply those time blocks across into their real diary.

It's important to note that not all months are equal in duration, and on occasion, a little flexibility will need to be applied (e.g. February is a short month).

By using this approach, your own diary can become reasonably predictable for months in advance, and when you get real tasks to overlay, you'll know exactly where they 'should' go rather than randomly assigning any open time.

As with every system, it is not designed to be overly restrictive, and a general guide of 'sliding tiles' can help you manage this whilst getting used to it.

To explain the concept of 'sliding tiles', I'm going to remind you of a toy you may well have enjoyed as a child. In the example image below, you can see a puzzle game where the aim is to make the picture of the elephant by sliding the tiles around. In this case the image has been completed correctly.

When it comes to your 'balanced diary', the tiles are the time blocks. The principle is simple:

'It's ok to move the tiles around to make life manageable, and to line up with when you want to do that task or to suit your situation week to week. However, what isn't ok is to create an elephant with no head but six legs by swapping the tasks out for others.'

That is, you shouldn't (very often) remove the balance of your diary by over-writing the optimum mix of tasks and times you have identified through your planning. Once in a while is ok when a genuine crisis or unusual need arises, but the idea of the balanced diary is to create... well... balance.

There are some other benefits of creating a diary using pre-defined tasks. It can also prevent wasteful small chunks of time sitting the diary.

As an example, if you work in a sales setting, you may choose to pre-set times for sales appointments that abut one another in the most efficient manner. By doing so, you can offer set starting times to potential customers and avoid the wasteful gaps that appear when this is managed the other way around.

See the example opposite.

For version 1, the sales person had simply offered fairly random appointment times to prospects when an opportunity arose. What this has led to is what I would refer to as a 'bitty' day.

There are 'bits' that are rather wasteful – half hour chunks that are likely (without a very disciplined secondary system) to become absorbed. This might be a tendency to slack off a little, or to do a less productive activity that is of short duration by its nature, but it isn't likely to be as productive for the business as it could be.

	Appointment Approach		Balanced Diary Approach
	Monday - version 1		**Monday - version 2**
09:00 - 09:30	Team meeting	09:00 - 09:30	Team meeting
09:30 - 10:00		09:30 - 10:00	
10:00 - 10:30	Mr and Mrs Smith - appointment	10:00 - 10:30	Sales Appointment 1 - Mr & Mrs Smith
10:30 - 11:00		10:30 - 11:00	
11:00 - 11:30		11:00 - 11:30	
11:30 - 12:00		11:30 - 12:00	Sales Appointment 2 - Mr Jones
12:00 - 12:30	Mrs Jones - appointment	12:00 - 12:30	
12:30 - 13:00		12:30 - 13:00	Lunch
13:00 - 13:30	Lunch	13:00 - 13:30	
13:30 - 14:00		13:30 - 14:00	
14:00 - 14:30		14:00 - 14:30	Sales Appointment 3 - STILL AVAILABLE
14:30 - 15:00		14:30 - 15:00	
15:00 - 15:30	Mr Davis - appointment	15:00 - 15:30	
15:30 - 16:00		15:30 - 16:00	Sales Appointment 4 - Mr Davis
16:00 - 16:30		16:00 - 16:30	
16:30 - 17:00	Sales report for supervisor	16:30 - 17:00	Sales report for supervisor

By contrast, the second version has identified that a regular sales appointment duration is 90 minutes for this particular business and sales role and has pre-set the optimal slots. This has allowed for four slots (not three as in the 'appointment approach') to be pre-set. When prospects express an interest, the sales person simply says, 'Great, I have a few meeting times available currently (provides details) – which would suit you best?'

In the vast majority of situations, the prospect then chooses one of the times that has been offered, rather than selecting a random time, as will happen when the sales person says, 'I have a free afternoon then, what time would suit you best?'

This principle doesn't just work within sales roles (that is just for an example) but works really well when the appointments you are booking are with yourself! This approach of defining ahead the most efficient loading of your diary *really* makes a difference.

I use it myself, and when I first set it up, I actually saved myself 17 hours every month... more than two full working days a month and therefore more than two full working weeks every year! Ever wanted a couple of weeks 'back' or to work 'on' your business? The time is there – you just need to be brutally disciplined in managing your responsibilities.

As with all systems, it isn't perfect, and it takes discipline to apply and live by... but I have yet to find a better way to keep the range of roles and responsibilities in balance intentionally and by way of a planned approach.

KEY TAKEAWAYS FOR BUSINESS OWNERS

The balanced diary is one method of handling multiple roles and multiple responsibilities pro-actively. It's important, however, that you also find the tools that are right for your situation and your aims.

I have found the balanced diary to be effective for two reasons. First, it wasn't just a case of listing out the tasks I have to do. It forced me to stop and think. To consider whether the tasks I was doing were actually required, and if they were, were they required to be done my me.

Second, for the responsibilities that I retained for myself, it also forced me to consider the way I was using my time. What was the most effective mix of activity to actually deliver on the responsibility under each role? In some cases, it even highlighted where I was not doing that well and needed to be more focused and to allow time to be that way.

The point I am making is that the tool you use is not important. You can use Kanban boards, project management software, task lists, or diaries. You can retain or delegate the tasks. I really don't mind. It is your business, and your life, and as a business owner I firmly believe that the decisions belong to you. The key point I *am* raising, however, is about efficiency and intent.

Are you clear on what you are trying to achieve overall?

Have you defined the roles and responsibilities, and the time required to deliver on them?

Because, regardless of what you want to achieve in life or through your businesses, the one asset none of us can make more of is time. The way you use that precious resource really matters, and life becomes a lot more enjoyable when you have more freedom within it.

The same principle we applied when discussing team performance deserves to be applied to yourself.

Current performance = Potential - Interferences

(from *The Inner Game of Tennis* by Timothy Gallwey)

Time management, and a lack of clear personal or business direction are three of the most significant 'Interferences' I have identified in my time working as a business coach, and also in my life as a business owner.

I strongly encourage you to bridge those issues early and set some great habits in place to keep you on track... and feel free to select a different tool if for any reason you don't like my recommendation!

A LITTLE BIT ABOUT BUSINESS EXIT PLANS

Lots of business owners eventually want to exit their business, and there are many strong arguments as to why they should.

No matter how passionate you are, and no matter how engaged you feel with your work today, it is unlikely that you will either want or be able to work at 90 years old.

In fact, none of us know what is around the corner, and the greatest freedom is available when income is secure and time is our own.

For this reason, I recommend you start planning to make yourself redundant! Not in the sense of loss of employment, but in the sense of not being 'essential' to the business.

The third circle on our Business Star diagram is all about independence.

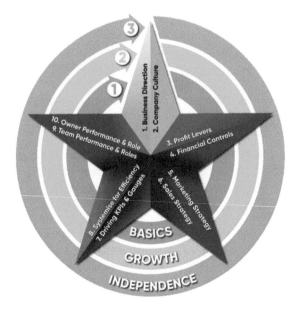

Whilst in earlier chapters we have spoken about this as a stage of progression, or of it aligning to wealth building and so on, the reality is that independence is also about security.

Your security is provided by a passive income, or a capital pay out. It can be enhanced by having more than you need to enjoy the fun things in life.

It is also about the security of your company, and of your colleagues too.

When a business is dependent upon you (or for that matter any other person), it is at risk. It only takes an accident, illness, or act of God, and it will crumble or at least suffer a strain.

Independence = resilience.

It's a goal to be aimed for when you want to improve your security, and it's also a goal that most investors look for when assessing the potential value represented by a company.

Is this business too reliant on the owner or any other member of the team?

Can it handle a change to personnel?

If the answer is that there is too much reliance, or an inability to easily adapt if the worst were to happen, the value decreases.

The last point I want to make about exit planning is that it's a good exercise to start early. There is even an argument that the only reason to start a business is to prepare it for sale, as none of us will be living forever!

Many company owners do not pay into a substantial pension and are too reliant on the monthly income that their business provides them.

Planning ahead for the exit, or at least for the future beyond your working years, is prudent. If your plan is that your business will pay you forever, plan for how that can happen without your ongoing involvement: passive or capital income.

Don't leave it too long before you have that plan in place, and even if you aim for that outcome, it's still wise to have a pension!

Chapter 13 – Reflection and Exercise

We have a clear organisational chart by role that shows all the OWNERS' roles and has their names assigned? **YES / NO**

Owners are clear on ALL the roles that are currently *reliant* upon them? **YES / NO**

Each role that they fulfil has a detailed and clear explanation of the responsibilities and related performance criteria for those roles? (sufficient to allow for easier systemisation and then for delegation) **YES / NO**

Each role has a clear set of reportable metrics, and a specified time and format for presenting those 'up' through the management structure (submarine management system) – even though this may be reporting to yourself at the moment, consider what you would need to see if the role were being fulfilled by another team-mate. **YES / NO**

Notes on low value / low difficulty tasks that need to be (or at least can be) systemised and made less reliant on the owner only:

....

....

....

....

....

....

Chapter 14

HOW DO YOU EAT AN ELEPHANT?

Whenever I have a big task ahead, I ask myself this question.

The answer is, of course, 'One bite at a time.'

But what does that mean in a business setting when we are looking at today but planning for the long term.

In Chapter 4 we looked at 'Business Direction', and we covered the principles of Objectives, Goals, and Tasks, as well as some of the tools and approaches that can be used to work up aligned plans. All good stuff and worth a quick recap before reading the rest of this chapter if you are still a bit fuzzy or need a reminder.

The reason I am referring back to that section is that one of the biggest challenges that business owners face is in achieving long term goals. This is because so very often their focus is drawn back to fighting today's fire – to responding to the immediate, or at least the short term. The stuff for today, tomorrow, and even this month always seems more urgent (and mistakenly more important) than the longer term distant outcomes. It can be hard, and take enormous discipline, to raise your eyes from the short distance to the longer term.

Henry Ford is quoted as saying:

'Obstacles are those frightful things you see when you take your eyes off your goal.'

I've always liked that quote as it instantly shows the danger of getting drawn into the short term alone, and the risk of finding that when you look up again, the goal has changed or moved.

As we said earlier, the purpose of your business should act as the North Star: a beacon to draw you on. As any sailor will tell you, however, if you take your eye off it for long, and then try and re-find it, it can take a few moments to re-orient.

In business, the equivalent happens when owners (and their teams by reflection) stop looking beyond the short term. They can easily lose direction and motivation, and then find themselves off their intended path by some distance.

It's your role as the business owner to keep periodically looking up – refixing the direction in your mind and ensuring others are still following. To do so, it's important to put a set of planning and direction setting behaviours in place.

My suggested framework is overleaf:

Create a powerful purpose statement and define the finished business vision

➤ Clarify the long term aim and the 'why' to emotionally drive it.

➤ Share this clearly and reference it often – the team should know it!

Define a five-year Big Hairy Audacious Goal (BHAG)

➤ BHAG is from Jim Collins' fantastic book, *Built to Last*. It's a concept that is easy to explain and easy for a team to align behind.

➤ Use this as a unifying theme for the next big step. I liken this to the flight navigation systems used by commercial airliners. They literally guides the plane to its ultimate destination, from waypoint to waypoint, even when that destination is far in the distance and out of visual range.

Set 12 month/3 year Milestone Goals (and a supporting plan)

➤ In the same way as that airliner knows the ultimate destination, it also has a set of clear milestones, directions, turns, and changes to make on the journey. Map out the course between here and there.

➤ Ensure that your team are involved in the definition of some of these goals. An engaged team is much more likely to support and feel part of the business if they have been involved in its creation and its direction.

Define an aligned 90 day Activity Plan

➤ Identify the steps for *now*, and make sure that they are progressing the journey in line with the bigger plan.

➤ Create a time-lined action plan, with personal accountability, that is highly visible to all. Make sure that the team is engaged, understand what is needed, and are committed from the outset.

➤ Track progress and performance, and 'tack into the wind' where needed.

➤ A famous general once said, 'A plan becomes out of date as soon as it is made.' Make sure that you update the actions to ensure the outcomes... that is what matters most.

Weekly and daily planning and time management

➤ Make sure that your diary has time allowed for completing the tasks assigned.

➤ Use diaries, planning tools, and other resources to ensure that your 'on the business' projects are tracked and progressed just as diligently as the ones you complete for clients.

➤ Remember, you are the number one client of your own business. If it doesn't deliver for you overall, it isn't doing the job right!

Chapter 14 – Reflection and Exercise

We have a powerful purpose statement and finished business vision which is shared with the team. **YES / NO**

We have a five-year Big Hairy Audacious Goal (BHAG) – this is shared with the team. **YES / NO**

The business has clear milestone goals and plans (12 month / 3 year) **YES / NO**

The owners and team have clear personal development goals and plans **YES / NO**

The business (and where relevant each team) has a clear 90 day action plan

SMART Goals?   **YES / NO**

Timeline?   **YES / NO**

Clear accountability?   **YES / NO**

Tracking and regular progress reviews?   **YES / NO**

Business Owner(s) and other key staff members have a detailed Balanced Diary (or other effective system for ALL roles) to help manage the multiple roles, responsibilities, and tasks efficiently? **YES / NO**

OTHER NOTES:

....

....

....

....

Chapter 15

WHAT TO DO IF YOU NEED SOME HELP

Within this book we have covered a *lot*!

Some areas we have looked at with a degree of fine detail, and for others we have scratched the surface by sharing the principles only.

To have gone into full detail on everything would have made the creation of this book untenable. There are literally thousands, if not millions of books on business, and that list grows by the day.

When we first set out to write this book, however, we identified that most owners of SME companies are 'time poor' but enthusiasm rich.

We decided to focus in on providing a quick reference tool that would share some of the ideas, concepts, and tools that we have found most useful to our own businesses and to the clients we have served over the years.

Of course there is more involved.

A LOT MORE

And now you have a choice to make...

We hope that there are several elements of this book that will help you – if not instantly, then at least quickly. We hope that you are able to take and use them now and in the future with a degree of confidence and with a fresh way of thinking about the subjects they relate to.

What we also know for a fact is that this book alone will not answer all the questions you will have, and it will not directly change the results you are getting or will achieve moving forward. For that to happen, the theory needs to become activity. No great idea ever changed the world without action.

Which brings us back to your choice...

Do you want to do it alone, or do you want some help?

If you've enjoyed the book and can see value in the concepts and the approaches, but also see that having some **support to apply them** would be beneficial, then we'd love to hear from you. We and our teams are ready and willing to help you.

You can reach us on the contact details below:

Tim Rylatt	Henry Laker
Business Coaching	Marketing Support
UK Growth Coach	Growth by Design
tim@growthcoach.co.uk	henry@growth-by-design.co.uk
www.growthcoach.co.uk	www.growth-by-design.co.uk

About the Authors

ABOUT THE AUTHORS

TIM RYLATT

Tim has won the 'Best Client Results' award five times during his business coaching career, and is known for his pragmatic, strategic approach to solving company problems and empowering business owners.

In 2018, the marketing agency he founded with co-director Henry Laker also won the 'Best New Business' award for the Gatwick Diamond area.

Tim's work has been published in multiple business media, and he is a regular speaker at both online webinars and offline events. His presenting style is insightful, fun, and engaging!

Trained through the world's largest business coaching firm for a decade, Tim has enjoyed learning directly from many high profile business advisers including Marshall Goldsmith, Michael Heppell, Miles Downey, Brad Sugars, and many more.

Now running an independent coaching firm, UK Growth Coach, Tim is known for his direct and friendly nature and an unwavering focus on delivering results. He likes to drive change in people and companies, and creates energy within those he works with – both in his own businesses and those of clients.

Tim is a highly experienced coach (having worked with

around 200 companies), and this is underpinned by a solid and qualified background in training from a prior career within two police forces.

On a personal level, Tim has a passionate interest in understanding what motivates people and the science behind performance. His two books (Business Battleships, 2012 and Growing by Design, 2019) focus on the reasons behind customer behaviour in the setting of marketing and sales.

Tim really enjoys working with the owners of SMEs. He helps them make the big leap from 'owning their own job' to having a company that can 'run without them'. He takes great pleasure in helping them reclaim control, create personal work/life balance escaping the ties of their businesses, and in creating situations that allow them either a passive income or a valuable sale of their company if desired.

Tim is married to Juliet, whom he loves to travel the world with, and they are both avid movie fans!

Learn more at www.growthcoach.co.uk

HENRY LAKER

 Henry is a highly experienced business owner and has been heading up businesses within the print, design, and digital marketing sector for nearly 25 years. He is known for being entertaining, direct, and creative, with a huge passion for results-focused marketing creations.

In 2018, the marketing agency he founded with co-director Tim Rylatt won the 'Best New Business' award for the Gatwick Diamond area.

Henry is a director of Growth by Design, MJS Media, and also of UK Growth Coach. He enjoys making business results happen and has a shrewd marketing mind!

Over the years, Henry has worked with hundreds of businesses, helping them to define their brand, differentiate their value propositions, and present their marketing messages in highly effective formats both on- and offline.

On a day-to-day basis, he can be found leading the team at Growth by Design and helping clients to establish marketing plans and assets that take them from marketing average to marketing great.

Henry is also now serving business owners as a business coach at UK Growth Coach and draws on his extensive personal experience in doing so. He specialises in marketing, sales, and team management.

Henry is married to Di and has two daughters: Jade and Dulcie. He is also brave enough to own four Jack Russell terriers and spends a lot of social time out exercising with them.

Learn more at www.growth-by-design.co.uk

Lightning Source UK Ltd.
Milton Keynes UK
UKHW020041090321
379994UK00008B/111